200 BEST

Ad Photographers
worldwide

D1223966

LÜRZER'S INT'L
ARCHIVE

Contents

Contents

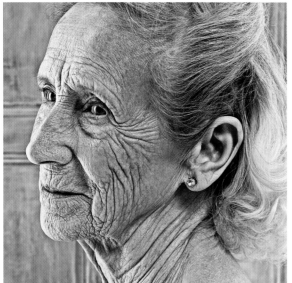

Two portraits from an Ogilvy & Mather Paris campaign for Dove. Published in 200 Best Ad Photographers 08/09.

Internationally renowned photographer James Day was part of the jury deciding what to feature on the pages to come.

Good photographers should be able to take pictures of anything well.

Based in London and New York, he works in advertising and editorial. He shoots for The New York Times, Time Magazine, Vanity Fair, GQ, and Wired on a regular basis and his images have been used in many award-winning advertising campaigns for clients such as British Airways, Harvey Nichols, Sony, Audi, and Heineken, to name just a few. In the past 20 years, many of these photos have been featured in the pages of Lürzer's Archive. His commercial work has garnered an extensive and impressive list of ad industry awards, including 50 awards from D&AD, including 4 Yellow Pencils. Michael Weinzettl wanted to know more about James and his stellar career in photography.

Hello James, first of all many thanks for taking part in the selection of work presented in this new volume of 200 Best Ad Photographers. What was your overall impression? Did any trends strike you in particular?
I felt that overall there seemed to be a slight move away from the over-use of post production and a shift to a slightly more naturalistic feel.

Lürzer's Archive has been featuring your work for almost 20 years now, most noticeably perhaps, on the cover of 200 Best Ad Photographers 14/15 with the image of the "grilling tarantulas." The earliest campaigns shot by you and featured in Archive were for Volkswagen and date around 2000 or 2001. Can you tell us about your beginnings as a photographer, and also how you got drawn to photography in the first place?
I began as an assistant aged 17 with absolutely no training whatsoever. Luckily for me, back then, if you could load a film back and a dark slide you were considered vaguely useful, and I was able to get a position as a 2nd assistant. Having left school a few months earlier under somewhat of a cloud, I will always be eternally grateful to the photographer who gave me a chance and taught me the basics. I immediately fell in love with it all and weirdly discovered that I had a reasonable talent for it. I assisted various photographers for about 8 years, most notably James Cotier, and then struck out on my own in 1996, which resulted in a huge overdraft and approximately four jobs that year. Gradually, with a lot of hard work, determination and a healthy dollop of luck, I started to pick some regular work.

Who were – or still are – your idols in photography?
My all time favourite photographer is, and always will be, the outstanding Irving Penn. The way that he was able to bring his mastery of lighting and composition equally to still life and portraiture was a huge inspiration.

You're especially well-known for your depiction of objects where, according to Communication Arts, you find "poetry from the most banal objects of daily life and extract the soul from a mere collection of atoms." Where does this interest in objects come from?

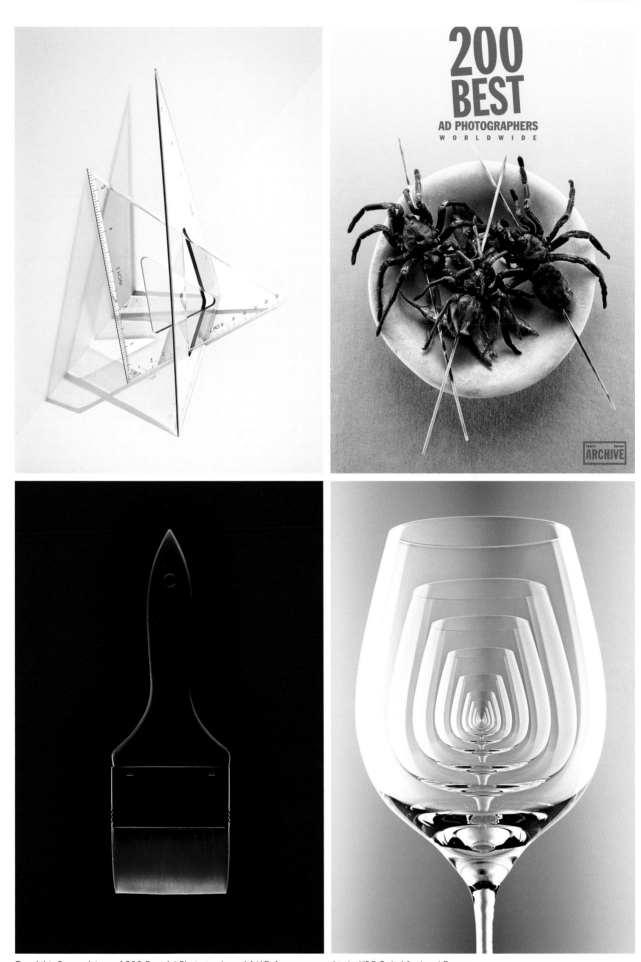

Top right: Cover picture of 200 Best Ad Photographers 14/15, from a campaign by Y&R Dubai for Land Rover.
Bottom right: A picture for DLKW Lowe, London, and Sunlight. Top and bottom left: Self-promotion. All published in 200 Best Ad Photographers 16/17.

Interview

I suppose that it was influenced initially by the fact that I trained under still life photographers. However, I have always been fascinated by the challenge of trying to elevate objects that at first seem dull and boring to something more sophisticated and elegant.

You have also worked extensively in other photographic genres, such as cars and portraits. Did you find it difficult to cross over? Sometimes advertising agencies want one specific style from a photographer and it's hard to sell them work that goes beyond the confines of a particular genre. How have you handled this?

I have been very lucky to be commissioned in all of those genres and yes, it is difficult to cross over. The car work was a natural extension of the still life, I suppose, but the crossover into portraiture was much harder to achieve. I think that once you have proved yourself with agencies in one genre they are much more willing to give you a chance to show them what you can do in another. Ultimately, I have always felt that a good photographer should be able to take pictures of anything well, but we all have a personal preference and style which doesn't always translate to all subject matter.

What is the work for advertising you're proudest of? The campaigns that won you all the awards (Pencils, etc)? How important are ad awards to you?

I am so proud of so many campaigns that I have been lucky enough to be involved in over the years, but if I had to pick one I would probably say the Harvey Nichols Calendar campaign. It was the first campaign that I won D&AD Pencils and Gold Lions for, and when the art director was describing the layouts to me I can distinctly remember thinking, "I'm definitely up for doing these, they sound amazing!".

When I was starting out, ad awards were super important to me and I can still remember the thrill of winning my first ones. They were very helpful in getting me noticed by other creatives and definitely helped to further my career. However, these days I feel that with the never ending march of Instagram and social media, awards are less important to the up-and-coming photographers of today. They are able to reach new audiences in a way that I could have only dreamed of ten years ago. That being said, from an egotistical point of view I still love winning awards. They also seem to be the only currency with which my parents could gauge any form of success in my chosen career.

How and where do you get inspiration for your work?

All kinds of places give me inspiration but mostly the worlds of art, photography and my family.

Photography for advertising is often a collaborative effort. What were some of the collaborations you look back with the fondest memories, and why?

During my career I have collaborated with so many talented people whose ideas I have been lucky enough to bring to life. As the great photographer James Cotier once said to me, "Just make sure you work with the best art directors and your work will be amazing".

I was very lucky to meet Justin Tindall and Adam Tucker quite early on in my career. I have collaborated with them on some amazing, award-winning campaigns over the years. Justin was a very demanding art director to work with but I always knew that if he had chosen me for the shoot then he felt I was definitely the right man for the job. That was always very reassuring and always brought out the very best in my work. Although I was always gutted when he picked someone else, the results were always annoyingly excellent!

Which visual artist – living or dead – would you most like to collaborate with?

I would have loved to have assisted Irving Penn or, to be honest, just made the coffee for him.

What to you were the biggest changes ad photography has gone through since you first started?

Obviously the switch to digital has been a big thing over the years and also the advent of post production. As much as I love both, there was always something magical about getting the film back from the lab and seeing that somewhere amongst all the shots I had nailed it! There has been a big swing back to using film in the latest generation of photographers, which is great, but sadly I feel clients have become far too used to seeing everything immediately and on an ad shoot they feel very uncomfortable with the perceived risk of film.

What to you is a good photograph?

It is impossible to define a good photograph, although I'm sure there will be an algorithm for it soon. A great photo should stop you in your tracks and grab your attention. In this day and age, any photograph that can make people stop and take a moment to look is a good photograph.

Any advice you would give young emerging photographers who would like to work for the ad business?

Don't shoot what you think art directors want to see, shoot what you want to. If the work is good, they will come calling.

Self-promotion. Published in 200 Best Ad Photographers 10/11.

Top left: Self-promotion. Published in 200 Best Ad Photographers 12/13.
Top right: Work from a campaign for The Guardian with DDB London. Published in 200 Best Ad Photographers 06/07.
Bottom: Picture taken for an Ogilvy & Mather London campaign for Ford. Published in 200 Best Ad Photographers 08/09.

Pedro Jarque   Self-promotion

Dana Hursey   Self-promotion

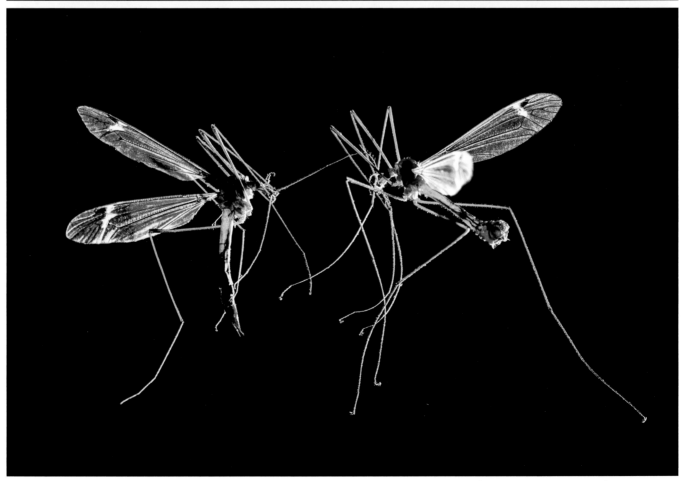

Christoph von Haussen   Self-promotion

Chris Frazer Smith We Are MBC, Datchet, UK Robin Horrex Bayer

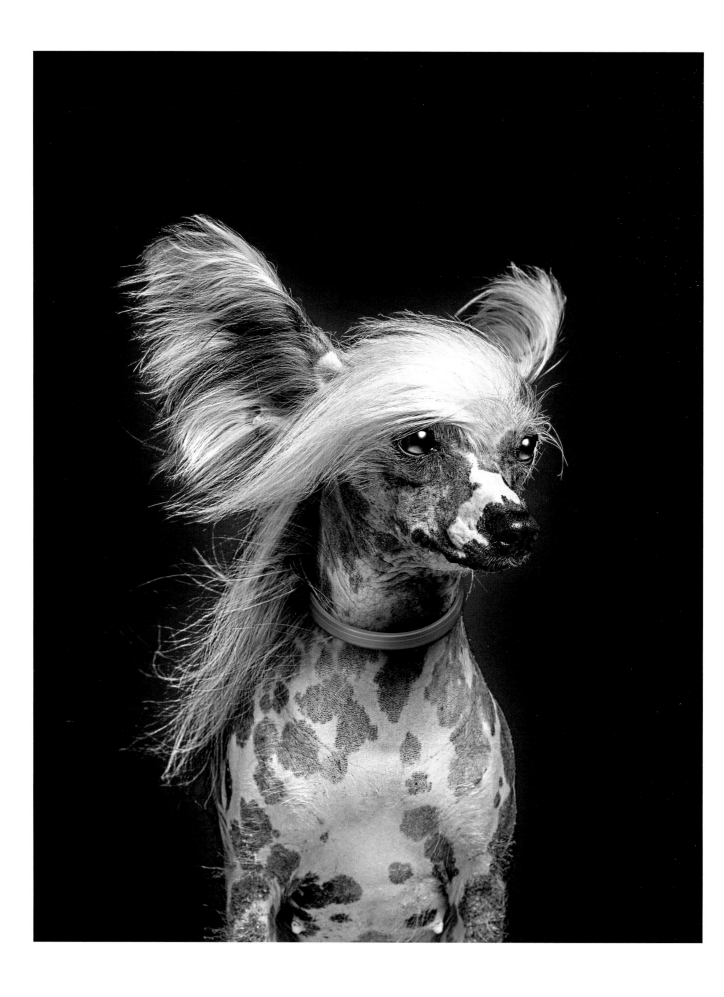

◎ Chris Frazer Smith ⌂ We Are MBC, Datchet, UK ✎ Robin Horrex ♙ Bayer

◎ Dave Todon
⌂ Rethink, Toronto
👁 Joel Holtby,
    Mike Dubrick,
    Aaron Starkman
✎ Joel Holtby
🖌 Instil Image Co
♆ Greenpeace Canada

◎ Jeremy Kohm ✎ Jeremy Kohm ☑ Architect Films ♔ Blue Ant Media

Zack Seckler Self-promotion

◎ Lennette Newell ♆ PetSmart

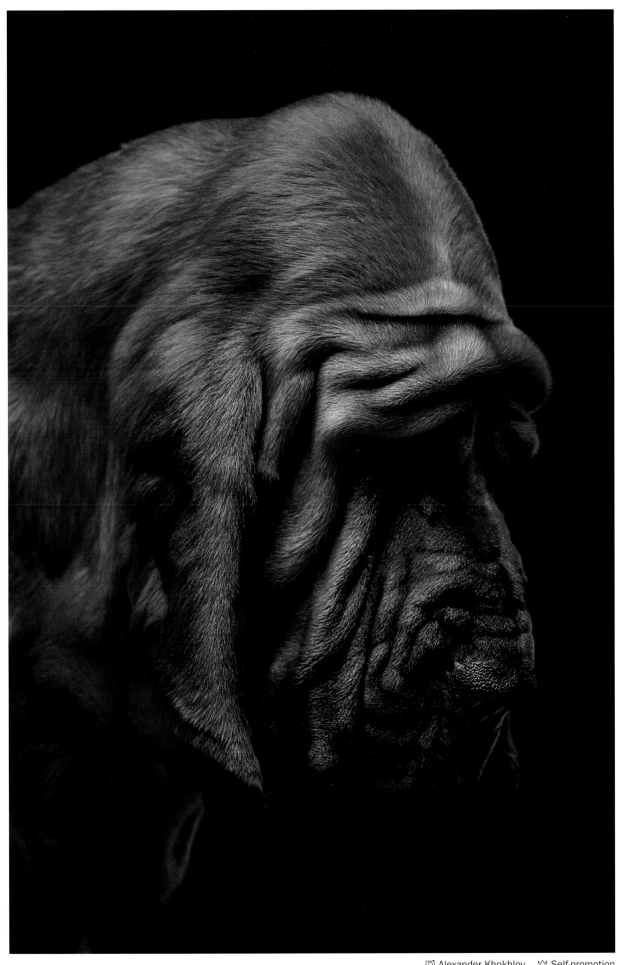

Michael Himpel   Self-promotion

◎ Joel Micah Miller ♔ Self-promotion

◎ Tim Müller   ৬ Self-promotion

◎ Tadd Myers   ⌂ Gavit Design, Dallas   ✎ Jessica Gavit   ✐ Jeff Whitlock   ♒ SH8 Merino

◎ Todd McVey   ✎ Todd McVey   ♕ Self-promotion

200 bph 20.001

Christo at the Serpentine Hyde Park, London.

◎ George Apostolidis   👁 Jill Kjluge   🏛 Cathy Apostolidis
🖐 The Mandarin Oriental Hotel Group

Architecture

☐ Erik Chmil
✎ Tom Stein, Zerone personal
♛ Self-promotion

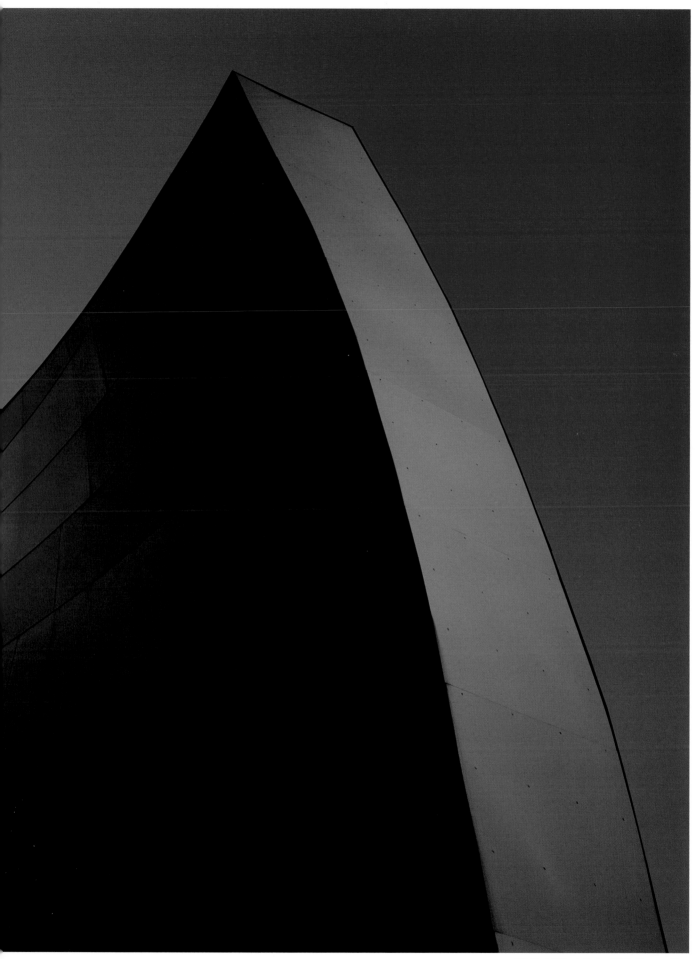

David Westphal   Self-promotion

◎ Rumi Ando ⌂ Amana, Tokyo ◉ Rumi Ando ✎ Junya Nagai ✐ Rumi Ando ♕ Self-promotion

Peter Oppenländer　Self-promotion

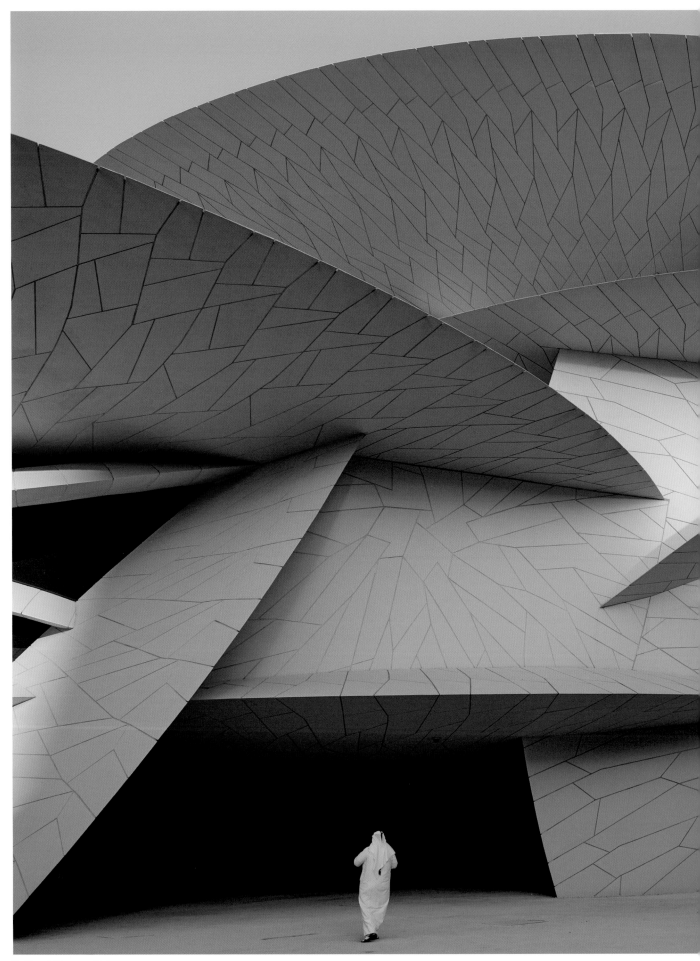

National Museum Qatar.

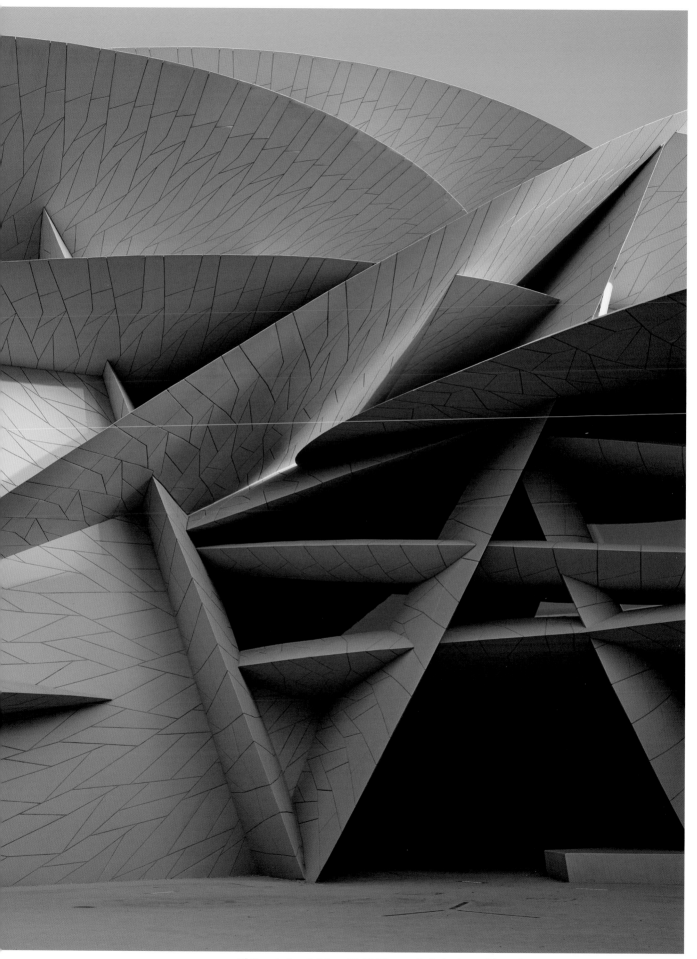

◎ George Apostolidis   ◉ Jill Kjluge   ⌂ Cathy Apostolidis   ♔ The Mandarin Oriental Hotel Group

Simon Stock   Self-promotion

Architecture

📷 Urs Bigler   👑 Self-promotion

📷 Urs Bigler   👑 Crossborders

☐ Kai-Uwe Gundlach   ⵣ Self-promotion

Julian Calverley   Turner's House Trust

📷 Joerg Schwalfenberg　　♔ Self-promotion

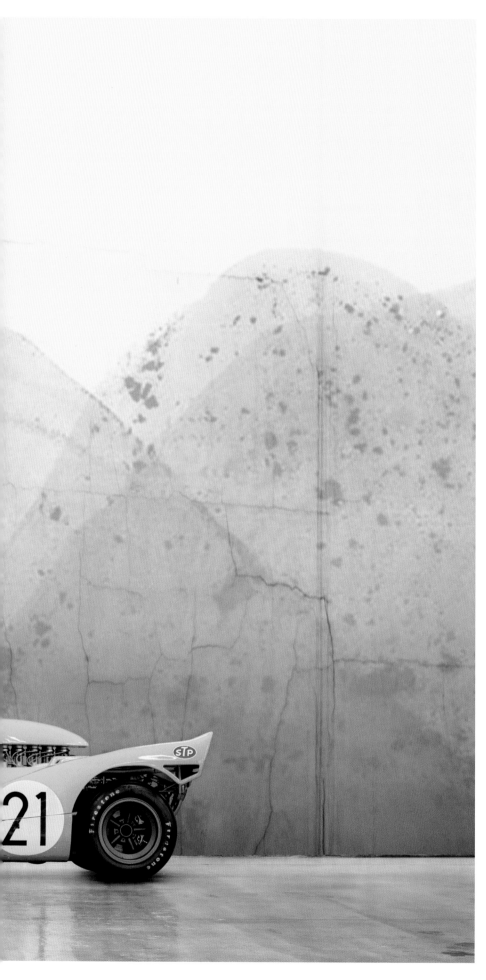

☐ Christopher Wilson
⌂ TBWA\Chiat\Day, Los Angeles
✐ Stacy Evans
♔ Nissan

◎ Bryan Helm   ᗐ Choppers Inc.

◎ Fraser Chatham ♕ Self-promotion

Eberhard Sauer   Self-promotion

☐ Graham Thorp   ⌂ Keko, London   ✎ Iain Ross   ☑ Recom Farmhouse   ♔ Bentley Motors

◎ Graham Thorp   ⌂ Keko, London   ✎ Iain Ross   ☑ Recom Farmhouse   ♔ Bentley Motors

⬡ Goran Tacevski   ☑ Studio d76   ♕ GLAD studio

David Westphal Self-promotion

◎ Sean C. Rice   ⌂ Racer Media & Marketing, Irvine, California   ⦿ Jarred Campbell   ✎ Laurence Foster   ⵌ Toyota Land Cruiser

Jeff Ludes
Self-promotion

◎ Lisa Linke   ☑ Gloss Postproduction   ♔ Self-promotion

⊙ Lisa Linke   ⌂ Keko, Frankfurt am Main   ☑ Recom   ♔ Porsche

⊙ Lisa Linke   ☑ Curve Digital   ♔ Self-promotion

Dave Todon   Self-promotion

◎ Tim Sutton   ⌂ Fluid Peak Collective, Idaho Falls, Idaho   ⵁ Nissan

Paul Ross Jones   Special Group, Auckland   Tony Bradbourne   Stu Mallarkey   Holden Australia/New Zealand

◎ Dejan Sokolovski   ⌣ Maserati

◉ Nick Hall   ⌂ JWT (J. Walter Thompson), Buenos Aires   ♔ Shell

Nick Hall   Gloss Retouching   Self-promotion

📷 Florian W. Mueller   ⌂ Self-promotion

⊙ Migs   ♙ Prestige Asia Pacific

📷 Erik Chmil   ⌂ Kemper Kommunikation, Frankfurt am Main   👁 Nadine Kubis   ✒ Recom   👑 Porsche AG

◎ Michael Schnabel　△ GTB, Dusseldorf　👁 Oliver Micklitz　♕ Ford

◎ Michael Schnabel　△ Delphys, Tokyo　👁 Yoshinori Nishimura　✎ Hideyasu Fujiwara　♕ Lexus

◎ Michael Schnabel　⌂ Delphys, Tokyo　👁 Yoshinori Nishimura　✎ Hideyasu Fujiwara　⌣ Lexus

Agnieszka Doroszewicz   Self-promotion

⊙ Anntheo   ⋓ Self-promotion

◎ Simon Puschmann   👁 Piggy Lines   🖋 Carnage Film   ☑ Mustard Post and Christian Cordova Bueno   ♛ McLaren

⊙ Simon Puschmann   ☖ Self-promotion

◉ Richard Thompson III   ⌂ Saatchi & Saatchi, New York   ◉ Alex Braxton, Jon Bellinger   ✎ Taylor James   ♔ Walmart

◎ Richard Thompson III   👁 Richard Thompson   ⚲ Richard Thompson III, Dmitriy Ten   ♛ Pagani Automobili

◎ Richard Thompson III   ⌂ MUH-TAY-ZIK | HOF-FER, Los Angeles   👁 Peter Neils, Miranda Lee
⚲ Richard Thompson III   ♛ Audi

◎ Stephan Romer   ⚐ Porsche E-Performance

◎ Stephan Romer   ⌄ Porsche Cayenne Turbo S E-Hybrid

◻ Frederic Schlosser   ☑ Frederic Schlosser   ৬ Self-promotion

⬚ Frederic Schlosser   ☑ Frederic Schlosser   ♙ Mercedes-AMG

⬚ Frederic Schlosser   ⌂ Innocean, Frankfurt am Main   ◉ Ricardo Wolff
✎ Felipe Cury, Marlon v. Franquemont, Sebastian Pattis   ☑ Frederic Schlosser   ♙ Hyundai

◎ Anke Luckmann   ⌂ LLR, Hamburg   ♔ Mercedes-Benz X-Class

◎ Anke Luckmann   ⌂ Team One, Los Angeles   ♔ Lexus

Anke Luckmann   DentsuBos, Montreal   Lexus

◎ Agnieszka Doroszewicz   👁 Julia Obermeier   ☑ Agnieszka Doroszewicz   ♕ BMW

Automotive

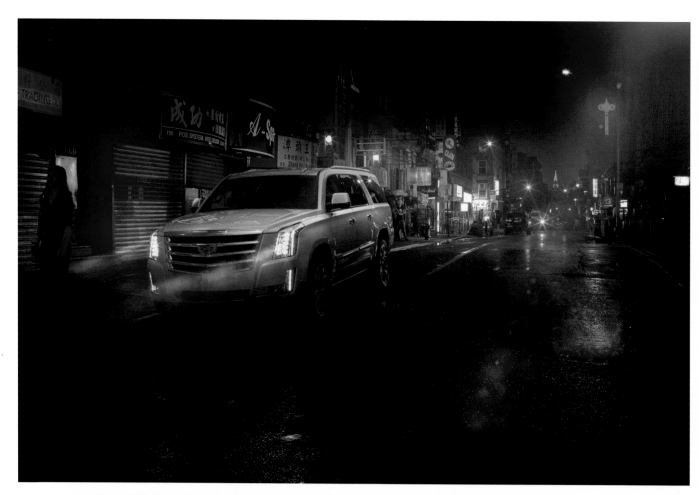

◎ Patrick Curtet   ⌂ Rokkan, New York   ☑ Curve Digital   ♔ Cadillac

Patrick Curtet   THE 25th FRAME Exhibition

◎ Aaron Cobb   ✎ Aaron Cobb   ♔ Southern California Timing Association

Kai-Uwe Gundlach   Self-promotion

Sam Bénard   Self-promotion

Andreas Hempel   Self-promotion

📷 Uwe Düttmann   ⌁ Self-promotion

Stan Musilek   Self-promotion

Stan Musilek   Self-promotion

Bernd Opitz Andreas Nimptsch Self-promotion

◎ Sam Robinson   ✎ Amy Fletcher   ♡ Beauty

◎ Arjun Mark　✎ Studio Lucid　🏛 Marianna Mukuchyan　👑 Self-promotion

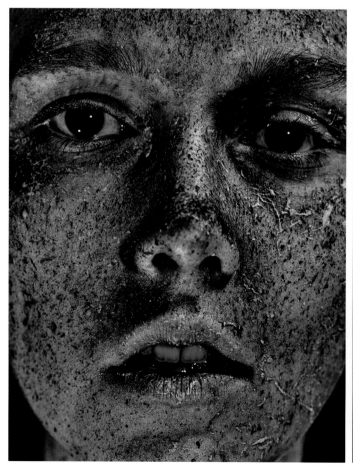

◎ Adam Black　🏛 Bianca Hartkopf　👑 Self-promotion

Klaudia Tot   Self-promotion

⬡ Steve Boniface　⬠ Colenso BBDO, Auckland　👁 Maria Devereux　✎ Emily Osborne
🖌 Jason King　♔ New Zealand Breast Cancer Foundation

Dana Hursey   Self-promotion

[camera] Stewart Cohen   [eye] Guillermo Tragant   [crown] Self-promotion

Jamie MacFadyen   M&C Saatchi, Sydney   Woolworths

◎ Callie Lipkin   ⌂ FCB, Chicago   ◉ Ciara Panacchia   ✎ Michele Morales   ♕ MilkPEP

◎ Mauricio Candela ⌂ Alma DDB, Miami 👁 Luis Miguel Messianu, Álvar Suñol, Juan Camilo Valdivieso
✎ David Álvarez, Luzalma Gonzalez ✐ The Blur Office ♔ Miami Dade Animal Shelter

◎ Frank Pham ♔ Self-promotion

Frank Pham Self-promotion

◎ Tosca Radigonda ♈ Self-promotion

Maria Schinz   Self-promotion

◎ Scott Van Osdol   ♔ Big Bend Ranch Rodeo

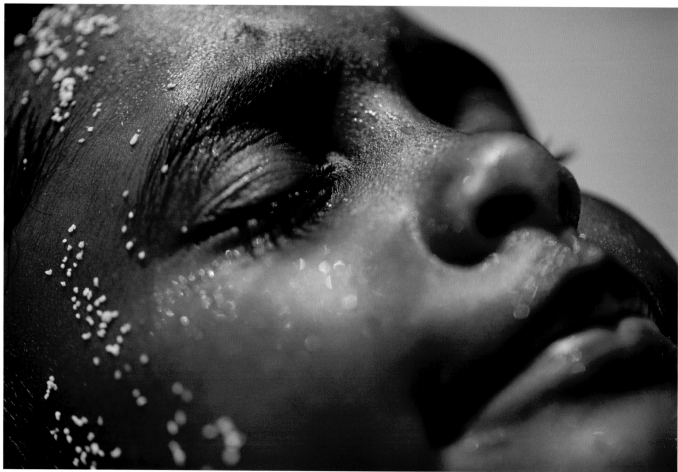

Sean Izzard   Host Havas, Sydney   Seamus Higgins   Gustavo Vampre   The Palau Pledge

◎ Wolf-Peter Steinheisser   ♡ Self-promotion

Bastian Görgens Self-promotion

◎ Braden Summers   ♕ Self-promotion

Erik Almas   Knight Agency, New York   John Logan   Kessler Collection

⊡ Erik Almas   👁 Amber Justice   ♕ Wonderful Company

⧉ Dean Alexander   ⌂ Design Army, Washington   ♔ Hong Kong Ballet

◎ Dirk Bader   🏛 Bernard Werkmeister, peopleandbrands, Marco Strucl   ♔ L'Officiel Hommes UA

⌖ Julia Keltsch   ⌂ Evelyn Innerhofer, Karin Postert   ♔ Latest Magazine

⊙ Tim Tadder ⌂ Natalie Bohlin ☑ Kozeth ♛ Glow

☐ Tim Tadder   🏛 Brian Coats, Benoit Moeyaert, Maki Hasegawa   ☑ Jana Heidenreich   ♕ HLA

◎ Lians Jadan   ♈ Self-promotion

◎ Jan Kriwol   ⌂ 2Koma7, Warsaw   ✎ Zuza Słomińska   ♕ Dilligent

📷 Jaap Vliegenthart   🏠 The Odd Shop, Amsterdam   👁 Niels de Wit, Jaap Vliegenthart
☑ Edwin Veer, Magic Digital Partners   👑 SUITE702

◎ Brenda de Vries   ⚐ Self-promotion

Brenda de Vries ♔ Treasure Hunters Amsterdam

◎ Stewart Cohen   ◉ Guillermo Tragant   ✎ Rafa Olarra   ⌂ Dallas Market Center

☐ David J. Fulde   ☝ Self-promotion

◎ Edo Kars ♡ Self-promotion

◎ Matt Hawthorne   ⌂ TBWA/CHIAT/DAY, Los Angeles   ⌣ Gatorade

Women in Town. | ◎ Maren Richter ♡ Self-promotion

📷 Mark Westerby   👁 Jonathon Brown   👑 The Gate

◎ Lewis Ho   👁 Jeremy Wong   👕 Harvey Nichols Hong Kong

Austin Walsh   Self-promotion

David Short　Jo Hawkins　David Short　David Short　Regatta

▢ Dominick Aznavour   ♕ Self-promotion

◎ Stephan Romer   ♔ Self-promotion

© Jamie MacFadyen   Self-promotion

Food & Drink

⟲ Julia Hildebrand + Ingolf Hatz   ☉ Birgit Schönau   ⤳ Self-promotion

Dan Goldberg   Dog Can Hunt, Greenough, Montana   Larry Lipson   Andrea Kuhn   Sunny Jin   The Resort At Paws Up

◎ Dan Goldberg
⌂ Dog Can Hunt,
  Greenough, Montana
◉ Larry Lipson
🏛 Andrea Kuhn
☕ Erin Quon, Sunny Jin
♕ The Resort At Paws Up

Dan Goldberg
Andrea Kuhn
Maria Del Mar
Self-promotion

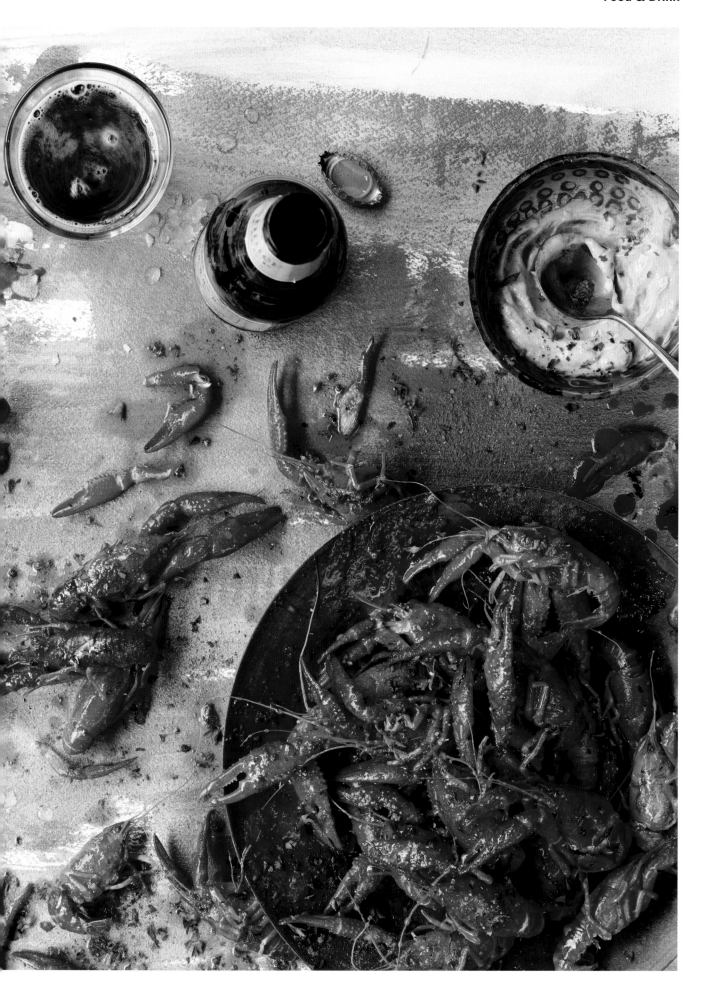

◎ Dan Goldberg
⌂ Andrea Kuhn
⊕ Maria Del Mar
♡ Self-promotion

◎ Theodosis Georgiadis ⌣ Mytilos

◎ Bruce Peterson   ✎ Toan Trinh   ⌣ Boston Magazine

◎ Patrice De Villiers ♔ Self-promotion

◎ Patrice De Villiers ♔ The Times

◎ Patrice De Villiers ♔ Harrods

Sonja Hofmann   Pinny Daniel, Raik Holst   Self-promotion

📷 Steve Hansen   ⌣ Self-promotion

📷 Daniel Ruíz   🏠 Dr. Marketing, Bogota   👁 Juan Carlos Parra   ✎ Enrique Gonzalez Wilches, Diana Gomez, Xiomara Martinez   🖒 LaPropia

⊙ Eduardo Wallace ⌂ Leo Burnett, Bogota 👁 Juan Romero, Mauricio Sarmiento, Luis Alejandro Mora
✎ Enrique Gonzalez Wilches, Yesica Charry ✏ Diego Chiliano ♛ Bavaria

David Stinson   Self-promotion

Food & Drink

◻ Nuno Correia   ◻ Lola MullenLowe, Madrid   ◻ San Miguel

Jonathan Knowles   Self-promotion

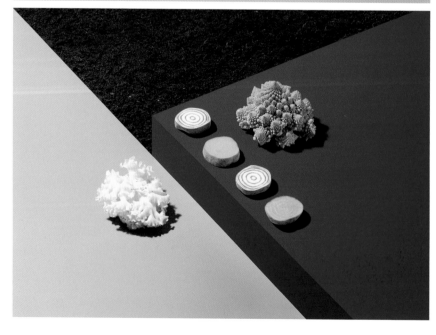

◎ Mikkel Jul Hvilshøj
⌂ Double Projects, Copenhagen
👁 Daniel Flösser
♨ Bite Copenhagen

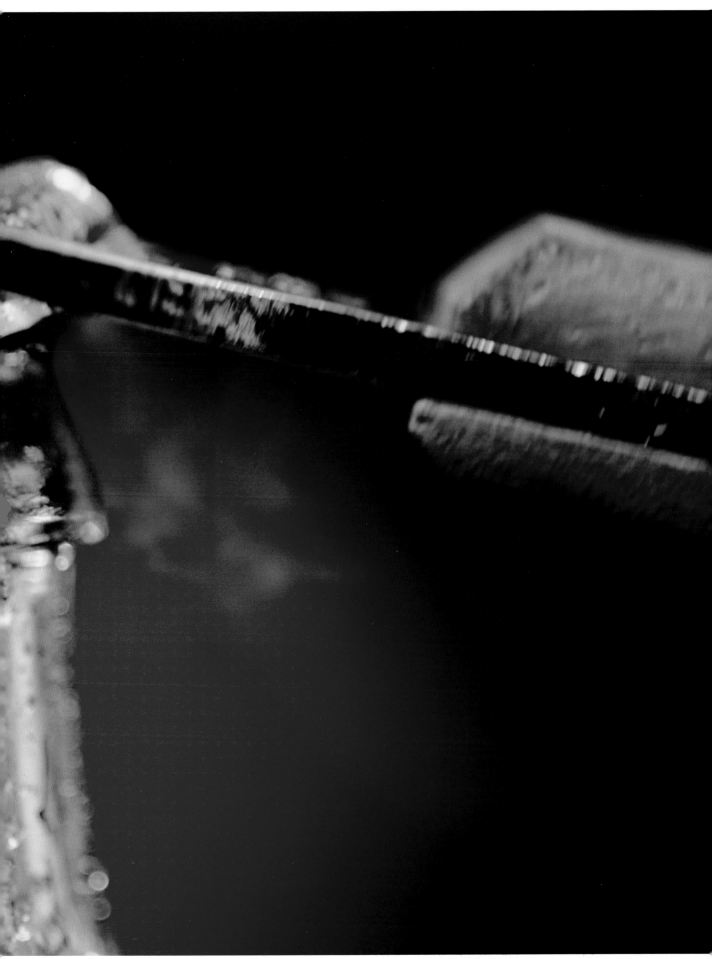

☉ Martin Wonnacott ♨ Coca Cola

◎ Martin Wonnacott   ⌂ BBDO, New York   👁 Danilo Boer, Marcos Kotlhar   ✎ Pedro Sampaio   ♕ Bacardi

Landscape

⬚ Uwe Düttmann
♡ Self-promotion

Landscape

📷 Simon Stock   👁 Jennifer Fox Freeman   👑 Gallery Stock, New York

📷 Simon Stock   👑 Self-promotion

◎ Dean West ♔ Self-promotion

☐ Tim Sutton   ♡ Self-promotion

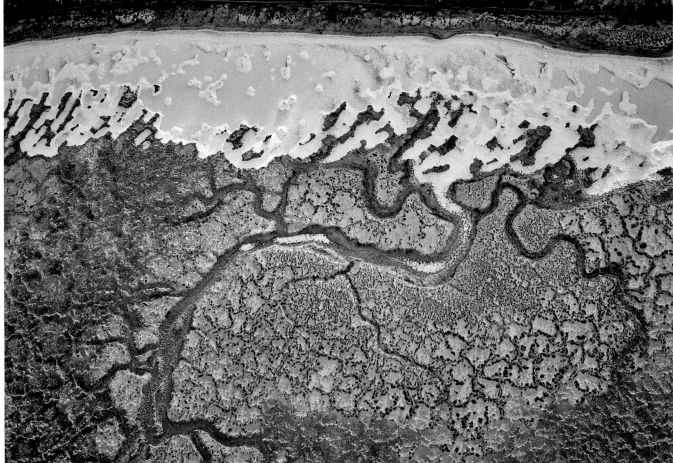

◎ Cameron Davidson   ᰃ Self-promotion

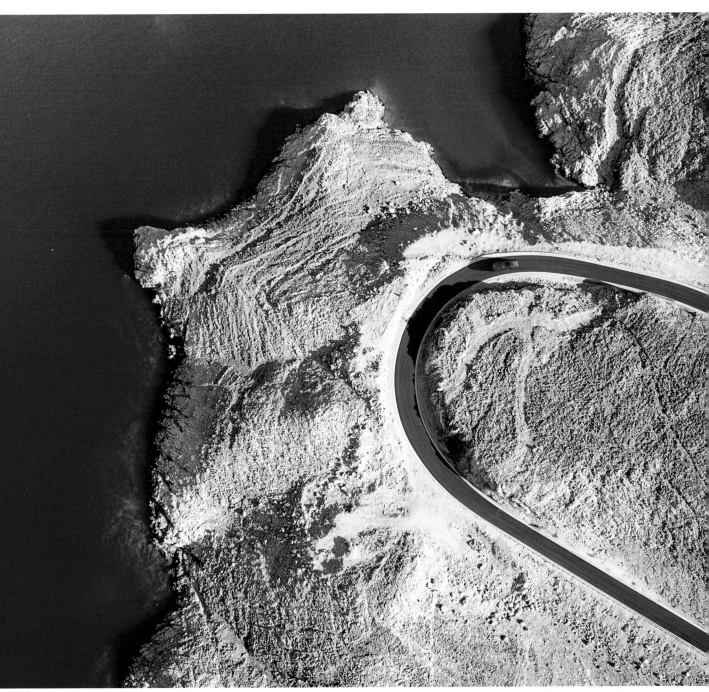

📷 Nigel Harniman   ⌂ Daughter, London   👁 Stuart Jackson   ✎ Phil Lynam   ♛ Rolls-Royce

◎ Simon Stock   ⌂ Pablo, London   👁 Tim Snape   ♈ Toby Carvery

⬚ Alex Telfer   ✎ Emily Graham   ✐ Jon Lloyd   ♔ Avaunt Magazine – Signs Of Life

📷 Dana Neibert ♡ Self-promotion

Christian Schmidt   Self-promotion

Landscape

📷 simon+kim   ✏️ simon+kim   ⌂ zb Zentralbahn

Stephan Romer   Self-promotion

☐ Tom Nagy ♡ Self-promotion

Thomas Bach   Self-promotion

⊙ Julian Calverley   ⌂ Spark44, London   ✎ Dan Delaney   ♙ Land Rover

Ty Cole   Self-promotion

Landscape

📷 Michael Schnabel   ♕ Self-promotion

📷 Michael Schnabel   ⌂ Taste, Frankfurt am Main   👁 Ralf Richter   ♕ Meckatzer

◎ Nick Hall ⌂ The Hilt, Seattle 👁 Bryan Cox ♕ Bristol Bay Native Corporation

◎ Nick Hall ♕ Self-promotion

◻ Michel Jaussi   ◉ Tom Rohrer   ✐ Salonen Postproduktion   ♅ Swisscom

◉ Michel Jaussi   ◉ Tom Rohrer   ✎ Salonen Postproduktion   ♔ Swisscom

◎ Julian Calverley ✎ Rupert Gale ♔ The Road Rat

◎ Julian Calverley ✎ Peter Schnaitmann ♔ Getty Images

◻ Julian Calverley ✎ Peter Schnaitmann ♔ Getty Images

◻ Julian Calverley ✎ Peter Schnaitmann ♔ Getty Images

⌾ Tom Nagy   ᗐ Self-promotion

Jason Lindsey   BVK, Milwaukee, Wisconsin   Matt Herrmann   Katelyn Tierney   Wyoming Office of Tourism

◎ Jason Lindsey ⌂ BVK, Milwaukee, Wisconsin 👁 Matt Herrmann ✎ Katelyn Tierney ♔ Wyoming Office of Tourism

◎ Jason Lindsey ♔ Self-promotion

Landscape

◎ Dirk Karsten   ♔ Self-promotion

◎ Bryan Traylor   ♔ Self-promotion

◎ Madhur Shroff   ⌂ Willow & Boots, New Delhi   ✎ Amardeep Singh, Ravi Narain   ♔ Trips Unusual

◎ Craig Moodie   ⌂ Floodlight Media, Adelaide   ♔ Boral Australia

Christian Jung   Self-promotion

📷 Jørgen Reimer ♛ Self-promotion

Landscape

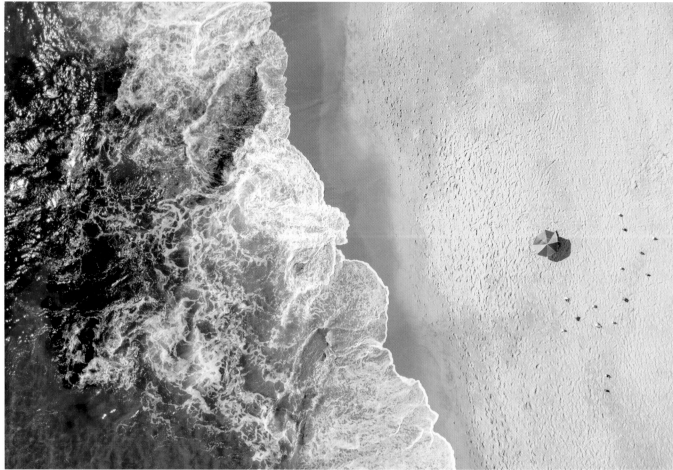

📷 Tracy + David   ☖ Self-promotion

Paul Fosbury Self-promotion

📷 Armand Tamboly   ♛ Self-promotion

Andy Mahr   Self-promotion

◎ Alex Telfer   ✎ Emily Graham   ✎ Jon Lloyd   ♔ Avaunt Magazine – Signs Of Life

◎ Alex Telfer ✎ Emily Graham ✐ Jon Lloyd ♕ Avaunt Magazine – Signs Of Life

◎ Alex Telfer ⌂ Philipp und Keuntje, Hamburg ◉ Deneke von Weltzien ✎ Boris Noll ✐ Jon Lloyd ♕ KWS

200 bph 20.045

◎ David Stinson   ♔ Self-promotion

◎ Andreas Franke   ♔ Self-promotion

◎ Jean-François Seguin   ✎ Freja Claesson   ✐ Peter Asbjorn   ☑ Erin Beveridge   ♔ Self-promotion

◎ Jean-François Seguin   ◉ Jean-François Seguin   ✎ Freja Claesson   ✐ Peter Asbjorn   ☑ Erin Beveridge   ♔ Sailing for Canada

Life

⬚ Todd Antony
♔ Self-promotion

◎ Karan Kapoor   ♈ Self-promotion

⌖ Niv Shank   ♙ Self-promotion

Jim Hughes   Self-promotion

◎ Erik Almas   ⌂ Young & Rubicam (Y&R), New York   ◉ Trevor Oldershaw   ♕ Crystal Cruises

⬚ Erik Almas   ᗡ Self-promotion

⬚ Erik Almas   ⌂ Grid Worldwide, Johannesburg   ◉ Nathan Reddy   ᗡ Visit Qatar

Garrod Kirkwood ♔ Self-promotion

◎ Matthew Joseph ⌂ Big Group, London ◉ Jane Linton ✎ Pierre Viger ♡ The North Face

◎ Terry Vine   ⌂ The Wood Agency, San Antonio, Texas   ✎ Kiki Lindholm   ⌣ Cordillera Ranch

Patrick Molnar ⬦ Self-promotion

◎ Christy Lee Rogers ♔ Self-promotion

◎ David Kelly   ♕ Self-promotion

⊙ Chris Straley   👁 Reid Thompson   ✎ David Boden, Heather Wines   👑 Hulu

Nick Hall   Self-promotion

Andy Mahr   Self-promotion

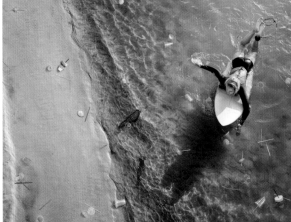

◎ Weston Fuller   ♆ Self-promotion

◎ Spid Pye   ✎ Spid Pye   ♡ Self-promotion

☐ Christopher Wilson
⌂ StrawberryFrog, New York
👁 Scott Goodson
✎ David Orton
Ⓨ StrawberryFrog

⌾ Felix Reed   ⌂ Combocut, Milan   👁 Sergej Grguric, Edoardo Scognamiglio   ✎ Felix Reed   ⌣ Costa Cruises

Kai-Uwe Gundlach   Self-promotion

Laurie Frankel   Wray Ward, Charlotte, North Carolina   Vivian Mize   Michael Hogan   Hilary Robertson   Sunbrella

◎ Alex Telfer   ⌂ 1751, Dublin   👁 Vaughan Yates   ✐ Jon Lloyd   ♕ Havana Club

Professor Linda Gask.   ◎ Alex Telfer   ✎ Kit Burnet   ✐ Jon Lloyd   ♕ Observer Magazine

◎ Marcus Kurn   ⌂ RBK Communication, Stockholm   ⊚ Erik Larsson   ✎ Erik Larsson   ✐ Johan Cabbe Cabezos   ♔ Miniumtech

Michael Mayo　Self-promotion

Life

◎ Todd Antony
♈ Self-promotion

200 bph 20.041

Teri Campbell   Self-promotion

◻ Jason Elias
♆ Self-promotion

◎ Christoph Siegert   ☑ Cathrin Bauendahl, Elektronische Schönheit
♔ Behörde für Umwelt und Energie Hamburg, Abteilung Naturschutz, Naturschutzgroßprojekt „Natürlich Hamburg!"

Andreas Franke   KNSK, Hamburg   Evonik Industries

◎ Martin Sigal   ⌂ Don, Buenos Aires   👁 Rafael Quijano   ✎ Diego Fernandez   👑 Cablevision Flow

⌾ Nicky Hamilton   ᵜ Self-promotion

Cotton House Hotel.

◎ Richard Schultz   👁 Alfredo Martinez   ⌂ Autograph Collection Hotels

◎ Tim Müller   ᗡ Wells Fargo

Life

⊡ Lisa + Remo Ubezio
♔ Festspiele Zürich

RJ Muna Liss Fain Dance

Lindsay Siu   One Twenty Three West, Vancouver   Rob Sweetman, Bryan Collins, Jeff Harrison   Jeff Harrison   Gabe Hall, Cristiano Correa   Vancouver Public Library

RJ Muna   Liss Fain Dance

◎ RJ Muna   ⋈ Flyaway Productions

⦿ Alexander Khokhlov ⌂ tbd, Zurich ✎ Christian Bobst ⚵ SVA Zürich

Ross Brown   Self-promotion

Andy Goodwin   Self-promotion

📷 Gerhard Linnekogel ⚘ Self-promotion

◎ Carioca   ⌂ JAZZ, Bucharest   👁 Valentin Suciu   ✎ Raluca Matei, Mihai Stoica   ♛ Orkla

◎ Carioca ⌂ JAZZ, Bucharest ◉ Valentin Suciu ✎ Raluca Matei, Mihai Stoica ♔ Orkla

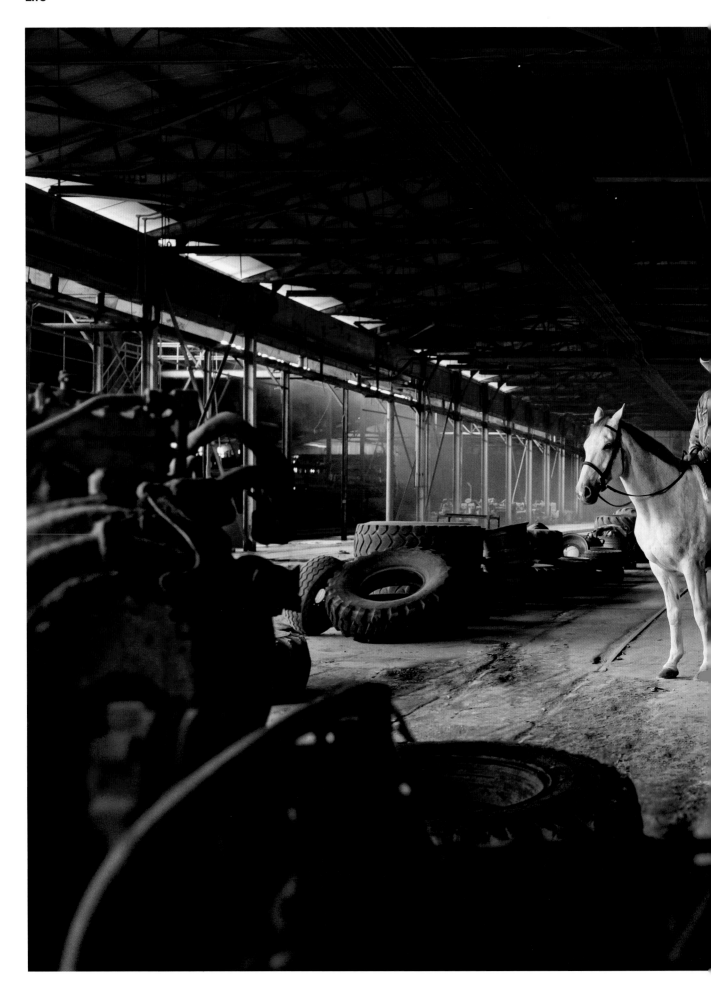

Bruce Deboer   Self-promotion

Remo Camerota   Self-promotion

◎ Darius Petrulaitis   ✎ Martynas Kazimierėnas   ♔ Self-promotion

Objects

◎ Laurie Frankel
⌂ Wray Ward, Charlotte,
   North Carolina
👁 Vivian Mize
✎ Michael Hogan
🏛 Hilary Robertson
♙ Sunbrella

⊡ Ryan Dyer   ⊚ Barbara Schmidt   ℮ studiobstyle   ☖ Star Tribune Magazine

◎ Ryan Dyer   ☝ Ashley Naum   ♡ Self-promotion

◎ Nikiforos Stamenis
♺ Self-promotion

◎ Tomoya Terada   ♔ Self-promotion

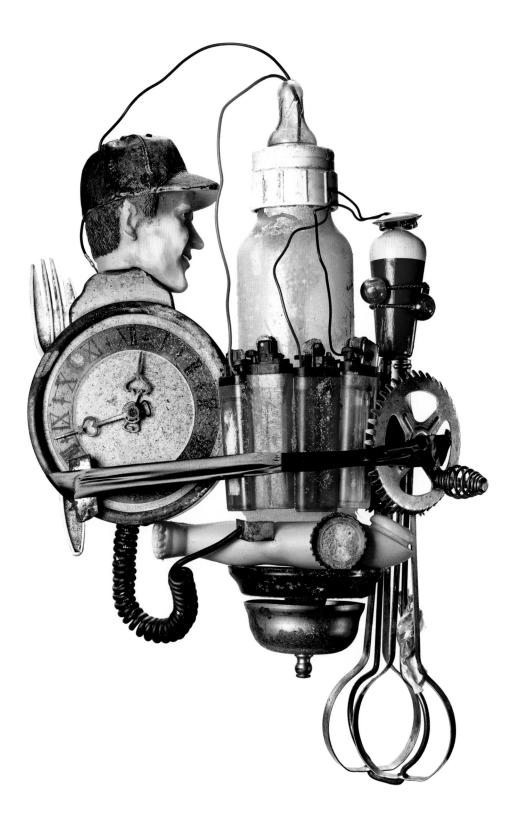

◎ Francisco de Deus   ⌂ VMLY&R, New York   ◉ Mike Wente, Harsh Kapadia, Silmo Bonomi, Gabriel Jardim, Guto Monteiro
✎ Gabriel Jardim, Shelby Hipol   ♺ Daryl McGregor   ⚲ Fuze Image   ♔ Lonely Whale, Point Break Foundation

🔲 Winfried Flohner   ✎ Andreas Wurm   ♔ Self-promotion

Adrian Mueller   Johannes Leonardo, New York   Annie Sterenberg   Megan Caponetto   Adidas

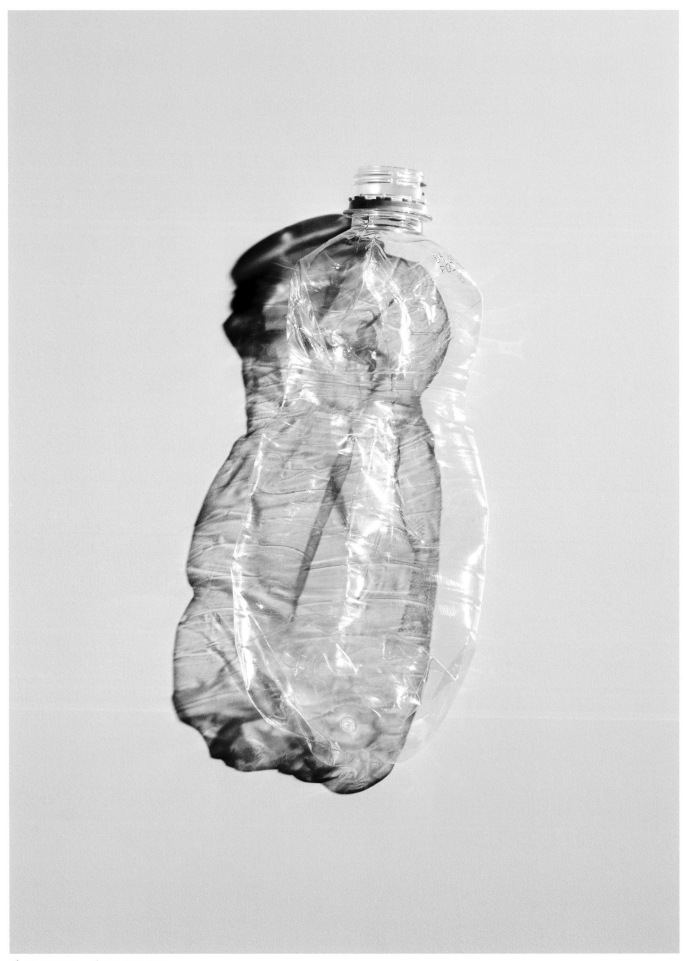

Kai Schwabe   Self-promotion

Re:Form – A Tribute to 100 years of Bauhaus.

◎ Olff Appold   ⴷ Art Exhibition stilwerk

☉ Jonathan Knowles　✎ Lauren Catten　✐ Jaina Minton　♛ Getty Images

Objects

📷 The Voorhes ✎ Tara Guertin, Jason Seldon 👑 Afar Magazine

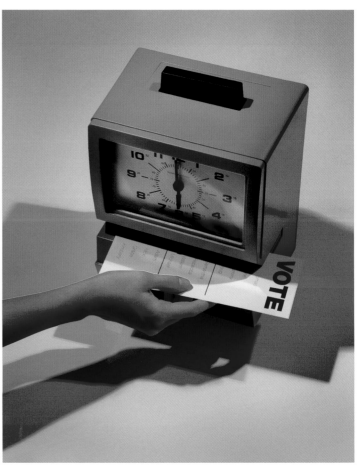

📷 The Voorhes ✎ Tara Guertin, Jason Seldon 👑 Afar Magazine   📷 The Voorhes ✎ Michelle Sulcov 👑 Glamour Magazine

⌾ The Voorhes ✎ Tara Guertin, Jason Seldon ♕ Afar Magazine

⌾ The Voorhes ✎ Tara Guertin, Jason Seldon ♕ Afar Magazine

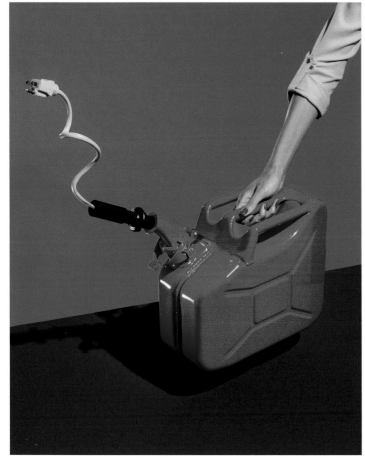

⌾ The Voorhes ✎ Tara Guertin, Jason Seldon ♕ Afar Magazine

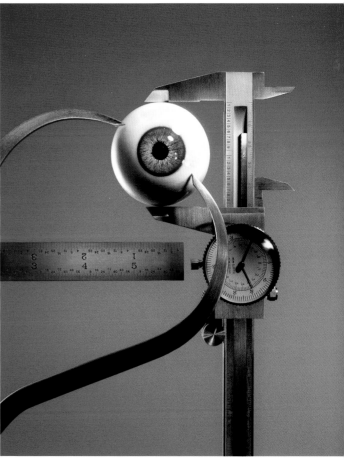

⌾ The Voorhes ✎ Chris Mihal ♕ Variety Magazine

Sebastian Magnani   Self-promotion

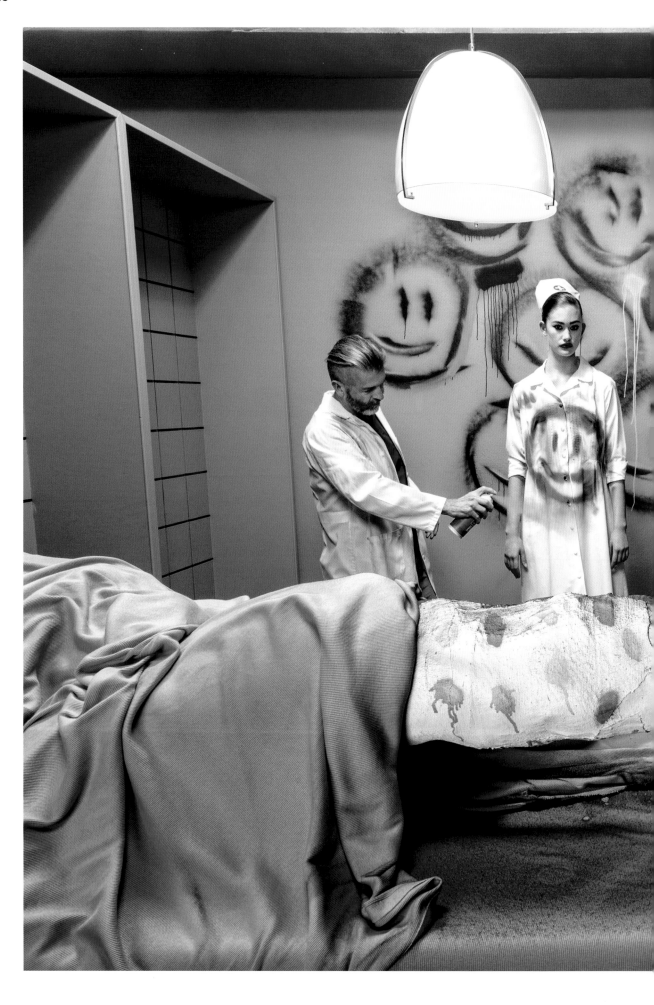

Stewart Cohen   Guillermo Tragant   Rafa Olarra   Dallas Market Center

◎ Laura Crosta   ♔ Trinity Yard School, Ghana

◎ Laura Crosta   ♔ Javier Dunn

Laura Crosta   Self-promotion

◎ Nano Cunha ♔ Self-promotion

◎ Antti Viitala   △ Boys and Girls, Dublin   👁 Laurence O'Byrne   ✎ Colm Coonagh   ♈ Jose Cuervo Tequila

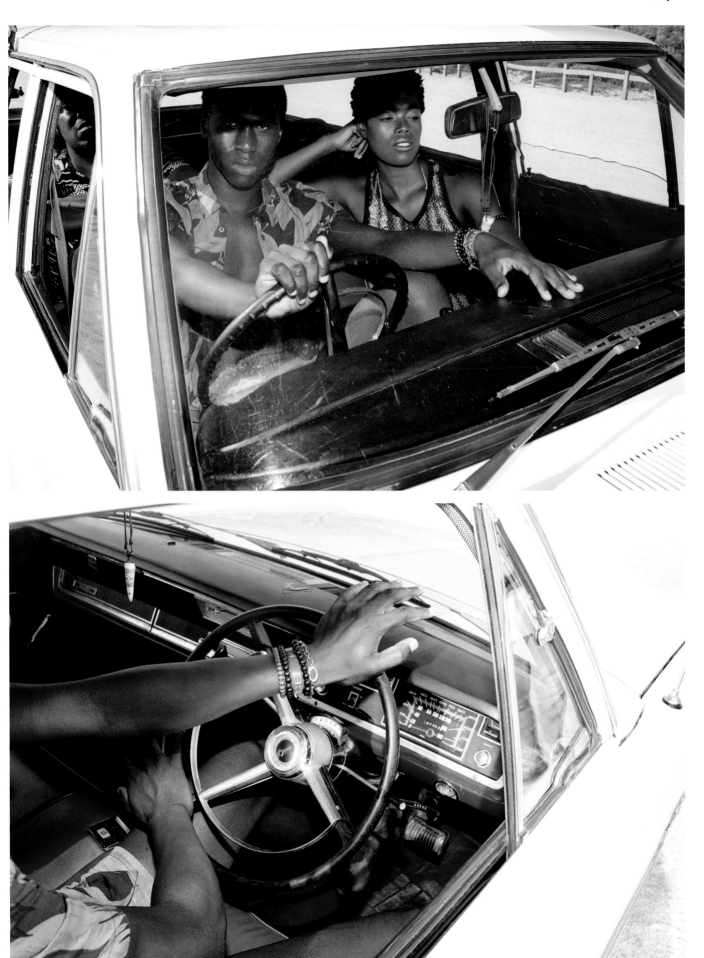

⬡ Anton Watts   ⬛ Robynne Kahn   ⬠ Self-promotion

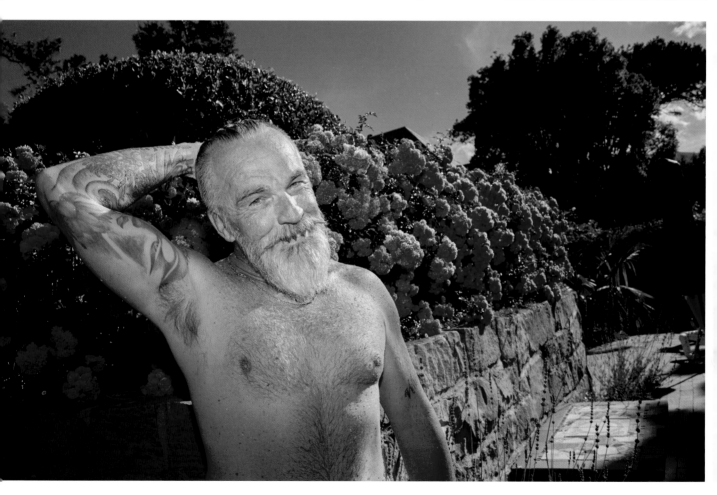

⬚ Uwe Düttmann   ♡ Self-promotion

◎ Brian Cummings ✎ Jurij Grdadolnik ♔ Self-promotion

◉ Yannick Wolff   ♔ Self-promotion

⌾ James K. Lowe   ♕ Self-promotion

◉ Simon Stock   ☝ BOXR Gym London

◎ Charlie Clift ◉ Charlie Clift Ⓐ Kate Forrester ᕼ Mental Health UK / British Land

Ralf Gellert   Self-promotion

Angústia Photo   Young & Rubicam (Y&R), São Paulo   Rafael Gil, Rafael Pitanguy, Rodrigo Almeida   Rafael Gil   Vivo

Paul Elledge   Self-promotion

Zach Anderson   Self-promotion

📷 Vincent Dixon ⌂ Arnold Worldwide, New York 👁 Icaro Doria ✎ Brunno Cortez ✏ Feelgood 🏵 American Red Cross

◎ Freddy Fabris   ♔ Self-promotion

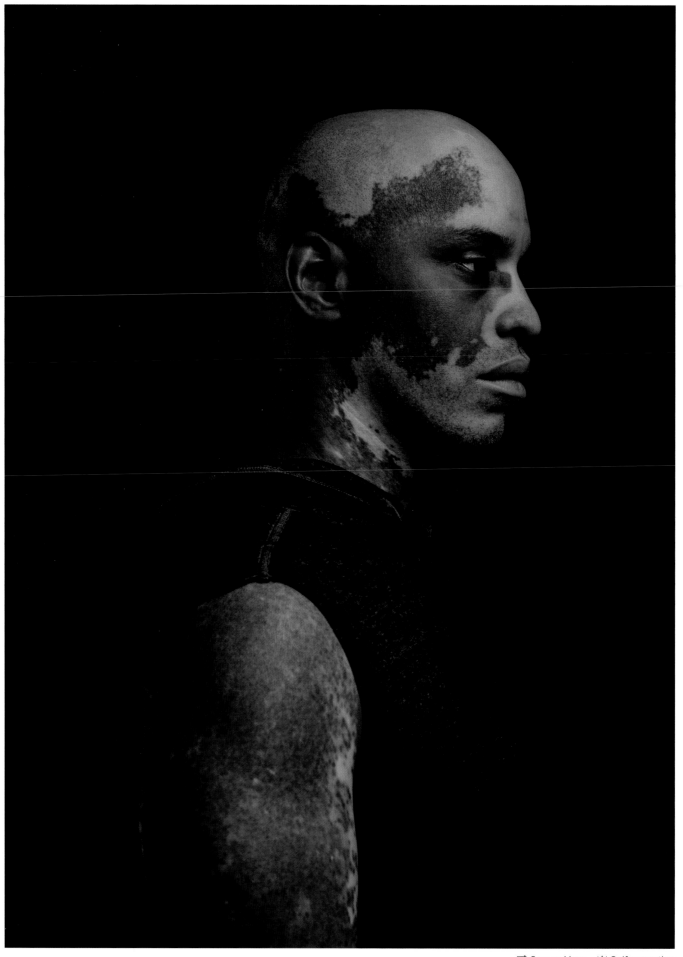

Caesar Lima Self-promotion

⌾ Lindsay Siu   ⌂ Cossette, Vancouver   👁 Katie Ainsworth   ✎ Gord Brown, Lisa Nakamura
🖌 Istvan (Steve) Pinter   🏛 Melanie Neufeld   ♕ BC Women's Health Foundation

◎ Chris Budgeon   ♛ Self-promotion

◎ Winfried Flohner　♔ Self-promotion

⌾ Mark Carter   ⌂ Self-promotion

Kremer Johnson   Self-promotion

◎ Lindsay Siu ✎ Istvan (Steve) Pinter ♔ Self-promotion

⊙ Lindsay Siu   ✎ Istvan (Steve) Pinter   ♕ Self-promotion

☐ Michael Heinsen   ♡ Self-promotion

◎ Bil Zelman
⌂ Piggyback Creative, Denver
◉ Leigh Masters
♕ Rio Grande Mexican Restaurants

◎ Florian Geiss   ♔ SOS Kinderdörfer

◎ Klaus Vedfelt ✎ Jesper Gregers Larsen ✐ Mogens Wittrup ♔ The Royal Danish Ballet

◎ Klaus Vedfelt ✎ Lauren Catten ⌂ Jane Marshall Whittaker ♔ Getty Images

◎ Christopher Wilson   👁 Jeff Campagna   ✐ Stacy Evans   ♈ Smithsonian Magazine

From the book
"Wiederaufstieg."

◎ Stefan Nimmesgern
👁 Arndt Jasper
♕ teNeues

◎ Márcio Rodrigues + Marco Mendes   ⌂ Young & Rubicam (Y&R), São Paulo   👁 Rafael Gil, Rafael Pitanguy, Rodrigo Almeida
✎ Rafael Gil   ✏ Rafael Gil   ♔ Plan Internacional

☐ Felix Reed   ♔ Self-promotion

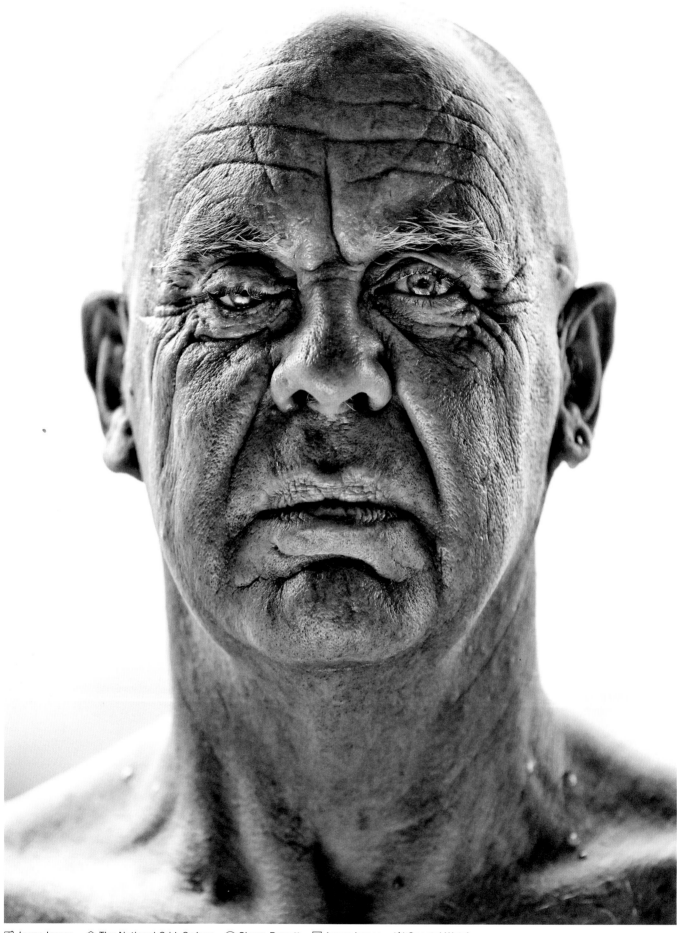

◎ Jason Ierace ⌂ The National Grid, Sydney 👁 Simon Barrett ☑ Jason Ierace ⌣ Coastal Watch

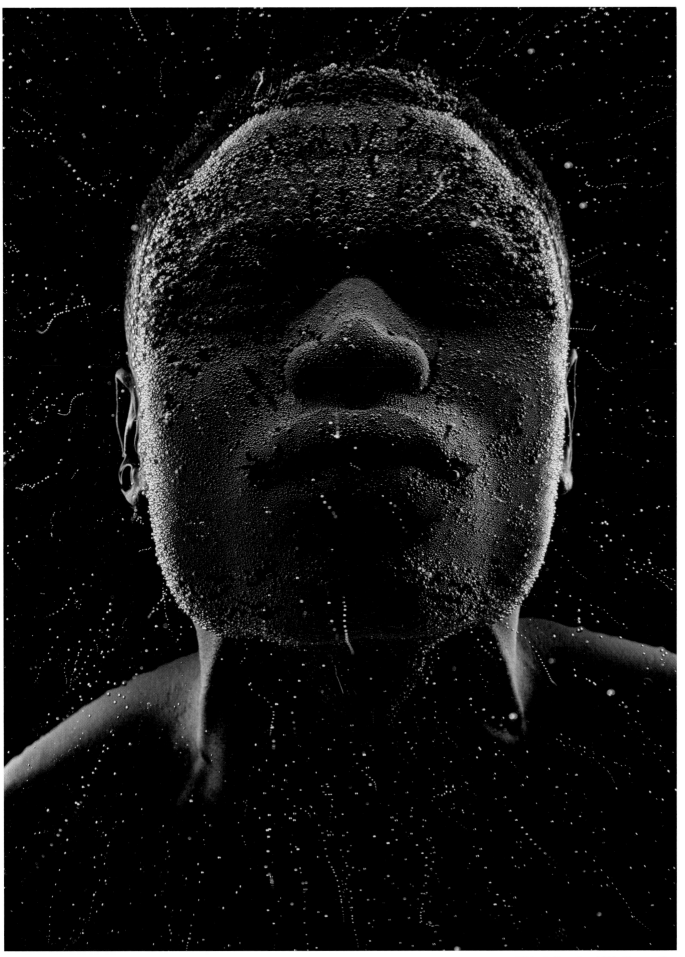

Jorge Puente   Self-promotion

Troy Goodall   TBWA, Singapore   SCB

⊡ Jonathan Knowles   ✎ Josie Gealer-Ng   ♔ Getty Images

◎ Hugh Peachey   ✐ Jason Riddell   ♔ Self-promotion

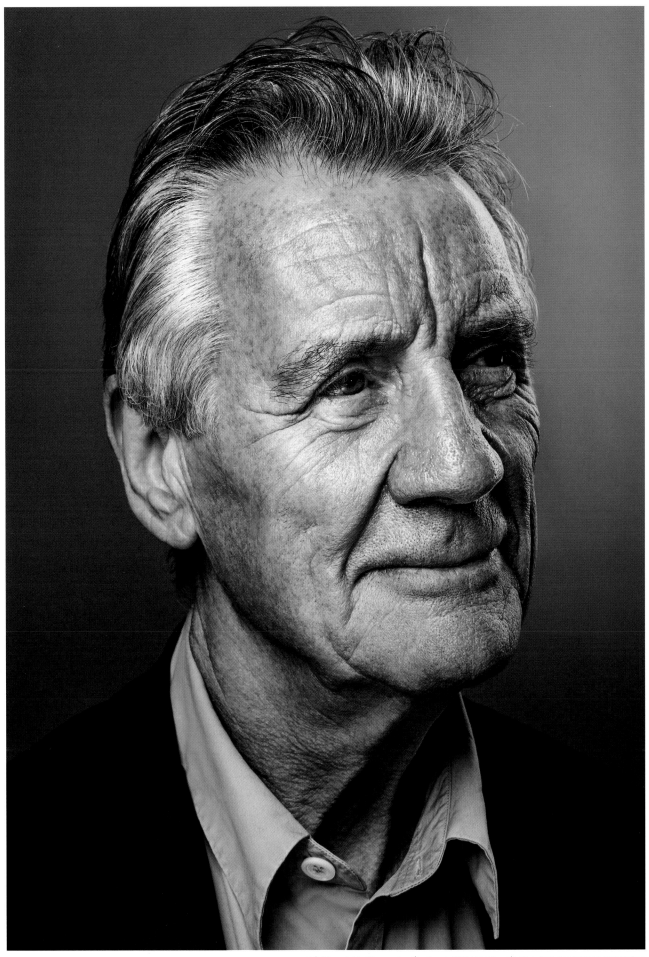

◎ Stuart McClymont ✎ Russ O'Connell ♔ The Sunday Times Magazine

Portraits

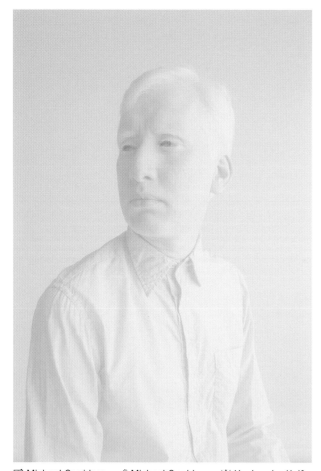

📷 Michael Corridore   🖌 Michael Corridore   👑 Husband + Knife

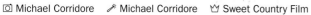
📷 Michael Corridore   🖌 Michael Corridore   👑 Sweet Country Film

Michael Corridore · Michael Corridore · Sweet Country Film

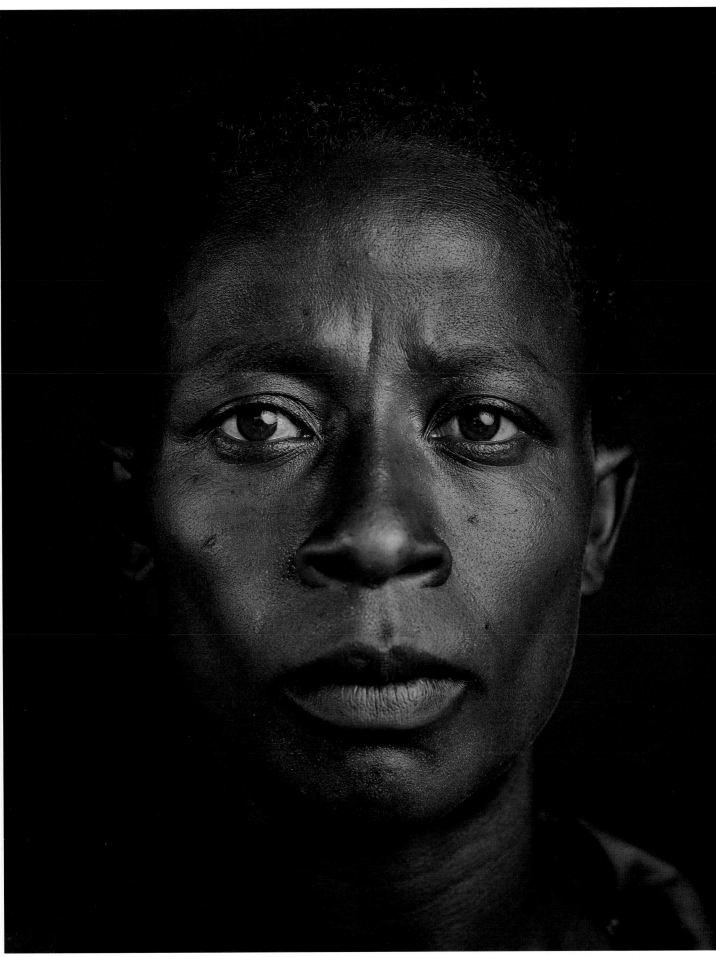

◎ Matthew Joseph   👁 Paul Matts, Matthew Joseph   ♕ ActionOnPodo.com

Mark Carter   MYOB

Tony Walsh, Poet. ⊙ Paul Fosbury   ✎ Dave Kirkwood   ✐ David Nightingale   ♔ Self-promotion

◎ Chris Frazer Smith ✎ Chris Frazer Smith ♔ Duckie, London

◎ Claus Morgenstern   🖊 Elmar Witt   ♕ Self-promotion

Portraits

◎ Art Streiber   ⴜ GQ Magazine

Art Streiber   Variety Magazine

Art Streiber　　Vanity Fair Magazine, New York

☐ Art Streiber ♛ New York Magazine

📷 Art Streiber   ♔ Entertainment Weekly

Art Streiber   Wieden + Kennedy, New York   KFC

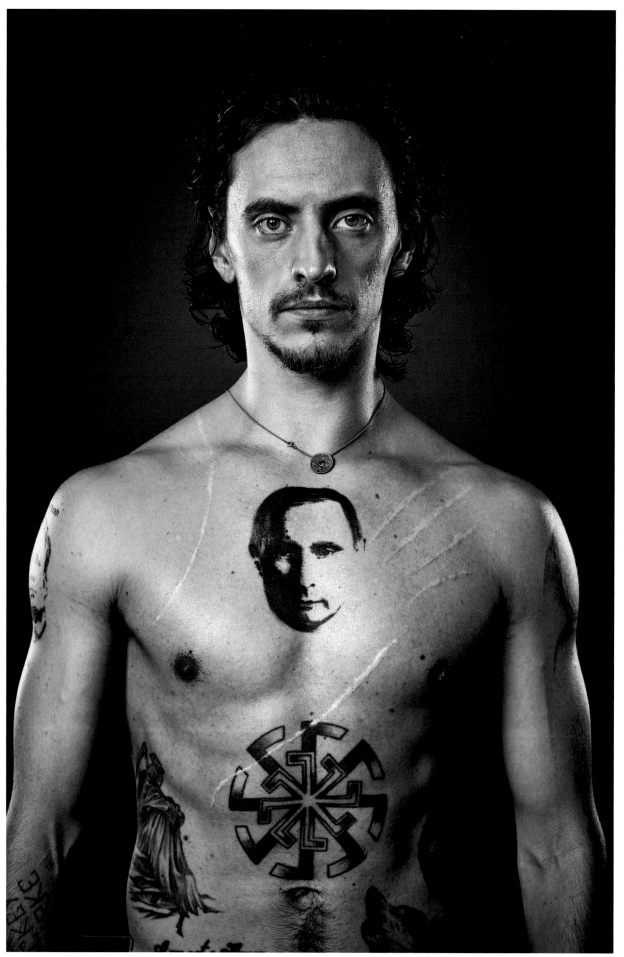

◎ Robert Wilson   ♕ The Times Magazine, News UK

☐ Stefan Sappert   ⌣ Self-promotion

Thomas Chadwick   View Imaging

Dominick Aznavour   Self-promotion

Sports

⊡ Normand Robert
☑ François Brisson
♕ Self-promotion

Tim Tadder Martin Morris New Era Cap Co.

Jamal Adams.

Kevin Love.

Tim Tadder　　Teresa McCarthy　　United Sports Brands

◎ David Salafia   ⌂ The Many, Los Angeles   ⊚ Blake Marquis   ✎ Zachary Williams   ♔ Biofreeze

◎ David Salafia   ⌂ Reebok, in-house, Boston   ⊚ Shawn Weatherbee   ♔ Reebok

◎ Rod McLean ♕ Self-promotion

Tim Tadder ♔ Self-promotion

Sports

◎ Stewart Cohen   👁 Christine Bastoni   ⌣ Lindblad-National Geographic

◎ Stewart Cohen   👁 Eric Moncaleano   ✎ Julius Prilianto   ⌣ Lake Austin Spa Resort

⬜ Stewart Cohen   👁 Ben Day   ☖ Baylor Scott & White Health

◎ Troy Goodall   ⌂ Clemenger BBDO, Wellington   ☖ The NZ Defense Force

◎ Hugh Peachey   ✎ Sterne Creative   ♕ Self-promotion

200 bph 20.013

Markku Lahdesmaki   Self-promotion

⌾ Paul Aresu   ♕ Self-promotion

◎ Sam Bénard   ♔ Self-promotion

◎ Derek Heisler   ♆ Self-promotion

◎ Normand Robert   ☑ François Brisson   ⤷ Self-promotion

◉ Sean Izzard   ⌂ Deloitte Digital, Melbourne   ◉ Charles Bayliss   ✎ Gustavo Vampre   ♔ Rebel Sport

◎ Teri Campbell   ◉ Ally McEwan   ♔ Procter & Gamble

◎ Oldbaby   ✎ Gabriel da Silva, Myriam Lopez   🏛 Santiago Rodriguez (The Black Shooter), Gabriel da Silva, Myriam Lopez   ♕ Self-promotion

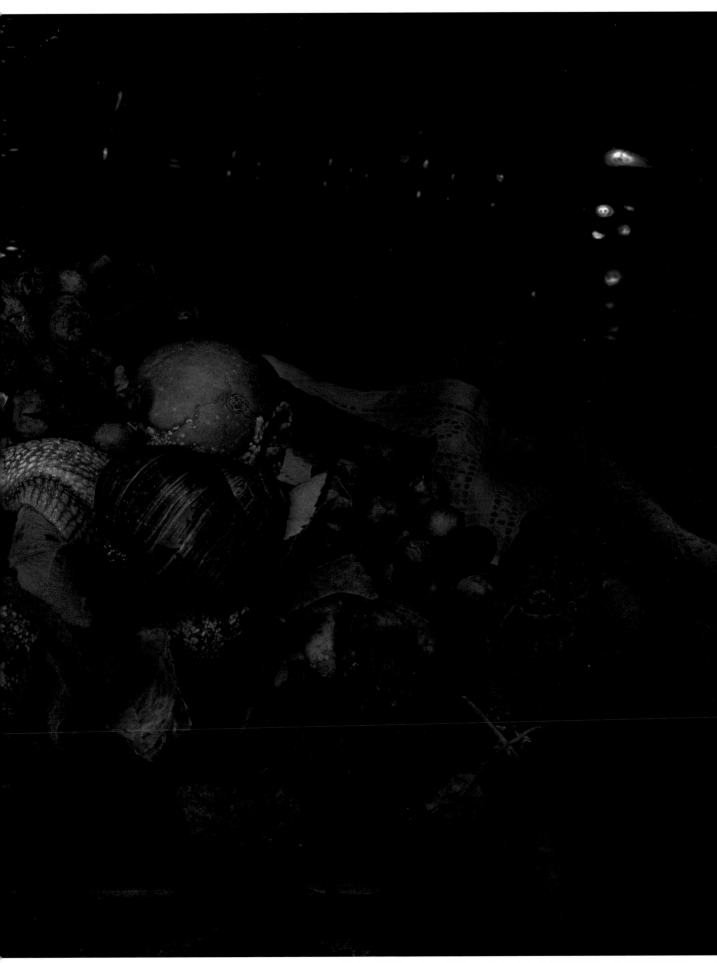

Jörg Schieferecke   Michaela Bazing   raff digital   Self-promotion

◎ Robb Scharetg   ✎ Jack Scharetg   ✐ Jeff Satterthwaite   ♔ Self-promotion

◉ Patrick Molnar   ♔ Self-promotion

◎ Robb Scharetg   ⌂ Harmonic International, Baltimore   ◉ Brian Fandetti   ✎ Brian Fandetti   ✐ Jeff Glotzl   ♕ MARAD

◎ Spid Pye   ✎ Spid Pye   ♡ Self-promotion

⌷ Ian Coble   ◉ Richard Pata   ✎ Ian Coble   ♙ Grundens

◎ Nick Hall   ⌂ The Hilt, Seattle   ◉ Bryan Cox   ৬ Bristol Bay Native Corporation

◎ Mac Holt ✎ Russell Shrewsbury ✐ Sergio Muñoz ♔ Western Towboats

Robb Long   Self-promotion

📷 Tyler Stableford ⌵ Patagonia Workwear

© Robb Scharetg   ♡ Self-promotion

John Fulton   Self-promotion

Work

📷 Andy Mahr   🏠 Art Society Global, Seattle   👁 David Edelstein   ♈ Liberty

📷 Andy Mahr   🏠 Craft Design, Manchester, New Hampshire   👁 Steve Richard   ♈ Timberland

Index

Cole, Ty
New York / Los Angeles
USA
info@tycole.com
tycole.com
Representative:
Brite Productions

Correia, Nuno
Nuno Correia Photography
Rua Carlos de Oliveira, no 3, r/c A
1600-028 Lisboa
Portugal
Phone: (351) 217 223 222
nuno.correia@nunocorreia-
photography.com
nunocorreiaphotography.com
Representative:
barbara.dias@nunocorreia-
photography.com

Corridore, Michael
Michael Corridore
Photographer PTY LTD
131 Nelson Street
2038 Annandale
Australia
Phone: (61) 417 659 966
michael@michaelcorridore.net
michaelcorridore.net

Crosta, Laura
USA
Phone NY: (1) 212 475 35 05
Phone LA: (1) 310 581 90 01
lauracrosta.com
laura@lauracrosta.com

Cummings, Brian
Brian Cummings Productions
USA
contact@briancummings.com
briancummings.com
Representative:
Amanda Björnson

Cunha, Nano
Estudio Nano Cunha
Rua Carlos Magalhaes 100
55 São Paulo
Brazil
Phone: (55) 11 96 177 37 06
nanocunha@nanocunha.com.br
nanocunha.com.br

Curtet, Patrick
M&P Curtet
Los Angeles
USA
Phone: (1) 424 316 90 44
patrick@curtet.com
curtet.com
Representative:
Cynthia Held
heldandassociates.com

Davidson, Cameron
Cameron Davidson LLC
Alexandria
USA
Phone: (1) 703 845 05 47
cameron@camerondavidson.com
camerondavidson.com

Deboer, Bruce
514 Daniels St. #343
27605 Raleigh
USA
Phone: (1) 646 202 17 70
bruce@brucedeboer.com
deboerworks.com
Representative:
Oryx Creatives
oryxcreatives.com

de Deus, Francisco
New York
USA
studio@franciscodedeus.com
franciscodedeus.com
instagram.com/francisco_dedeus
Representative USA:
bransch.net
branschnewyork@bransch.net
Representative Europe:
branscheurope@bransch.net

de Villiers, Patrice
Top Floor
5 Surrey Square
SE17 2JU London
UK
Phone: (44) 7774 133 849
patrice@patricedevilliers.com
eyemade.com
patricedevilliers.com
Representative Paris:
Eyemade
Phone: (33) 1 53 10 14 34
made@eyemade.com

de Vries, Brenda
Amsterdam
The Netherlands
Phone: (31) 626 154 909
brenda@brendadevries.com
brendadevries.com

Dixon, Vincent
USA
vincentdixon@me.com
vincentdixon.com
Representatives:
Brite Productions
briteproductions.net
Peter Bailey Company
peterbailey.co.uk
Mad For It Productions
madforitproductions.com
Ask Our Agents
askouragents.fr

Doroszewicz, Agnieszka
Steintwiete 16
20459 Hamburg
Germany
Phone: (49) 160 914 816 84
a@doroszewicz.com
doroszewicz.com
Representative:
Severin Wendeler
Christian Severin & Christian Wendeler
office@severinwendeler.de
Phone: (49) 40 800 80 99 99

Düttmann, Uwe
Uwe Duettmann
Elmenhorststr. 4
22767 Hamburg
Germany
Phone: (49) 40 866 00 666
ud@duettmann.com
duettmann.com

Dyer, Ryan
Ryan Dyer Photography
Minneapolis
USA
Phone: (1) 612 963 06 11
mail@ryandyer.com
ryandyer.com

Earp, Robert
Robert Earp PhotoMaker
19-27 Ireland Street
3003 Melbourne
Australia
Phone: (61) 413 535 045
rob@robertearp.com
robertearp.com
Representative China:
Ugly Duckling
annette@uglyd.com
Phone: (65) 62 95 18 33
Shooting Gallery
sebtan@shootinggalleryasia.com
Phone: (86) 21 6124 88 28
Representative Australia:
Fine Art
Black Eye Gallery
Phone: (61) 411 874 673
info@blackeyegallery.com.au

Elias, Jason
Venice
USA
Phone: (1) 310 251 63 09
jasonelias.com
Representative:
The Gren Group
thegrengroupinc.com

Elledge, Paul
Paul Elledge Photography, Inc
1808 W. Grand Ave.
60622 Chicago
USA
Phone: (1) 312 733 8021
studio@paulelledge.com
paulelledge.com
Representative:
Candace Gelman & Assoc.
candacegelman.com

Fabris, Freddy
Fabris Photography
1619 N Sawyer Ave
60647 Chicago
USA
Phone: (1) 312 401 13 24
info@fabrisphoto.com
fabrisphoto.com

Flohner, Winfried
Flohner Fotografie
Wetterbergweg 6
4203 Altenberg bei Linz
Austria

Fosbury, Paul
London
UK
Phone: (44) 77 888 180 11
email@paulfosbury.com
paulfosbury.com

Franke, Andreas
Staudinger & Franke GmbH
Josef-Endlweber-Gasse 2A
1230 Vienna
Austria
Phone: (43) 1 597 01 24
sf@staudinger-franke.com
staudinger-franke.com
Representative USA:
VISU Artists
Phone: (1) 800 979 84 78
inquiry@visu.co
visuartists.com
Representative Germany:
Kelly Kellerhoff
Phone: (49) 30 27 581 66-0
info@kellykellerhoff.de
kellykellerhoff.de

Representative Switzerland:
Marlies Lanker
Phone: (41) 44 361 70 09
fotografen@marlieslanker.ch
marlieslanker.ch
Representative UK:
Peter Bailey
Phone: (44) 20 7935 2626
peter@peterbailey.co.uk
peterbailey.co.uk

Frankel, Laurie
Laurie Frankel Photography
90 Buena Vista Terrace
94117 San Francisco
USA
Phone: (1) 415 282 73 45
info@lauriefrankel.com
lauriefrankel.com
Representative:
DS Reps
dsreps.com

Fulde, David J.
30 Merchants Wharf
M4A 0L2 Toronto
Canada
Phone: (1) 64 77 84 17 73
david@fulde.ca
fulde.ca

Fuller, Weston
Weston Fuller Photography
6965 El Camino Real,
Ste 105-153
92011 Carlsbad
USA
Phone: (1) 858 264 66 30
weston@westonfuller.com
westonfuller.com

Fulton, John
USA
Phone: (1) 805 637 10 43
johnfultonphotography.com
studio@johnfultonphotography.com
Representative:
VISU Artists
visuartists.com

Geiss, Florian
Mueggenkampstr. 31a
20257 Hamburg
Germany
Phone: (49) 40 46 00 56 50
info@floriangeiss.com
floriangeiss.com
Representative UK:
Horton Stephens Photographer's Agent
14 Peacock Yard
London SE17 3LH
Phone: (44) 20 72 52 79 79
horton-stephens.com
Representative USA:
Ray Brown Productions
601 West 26th Street, Suite 1310
10001 New York
Phone: (1) 212 243 50 57
raybrownpro.com

Gellert, Ralf
Friedensallee 126
22763 Hamburg
Germany
Phone: (49) 40 25 49 17 47
mail@ralfgellert.de
ralfgellert.de

Georgiadis, Theodosis
Theodosis Georgiadis Photography
Greece
Phone: (30) 69 45 43 88 45
theodosis@theodosisgeorgiadis.com
theodosisgeorgiadis.com

Index

McClymont, Stuart
London
UK
Phone: (44) 79 57 100 500
stu@stuartmcclymont.com
stuartmcclymont.com
Representative New York:
Janice Moses
janicemoses.com
Representative London:
JSR
jsragency.com

McLean, Rod
Anasara Productions, Inc
Vancouver
Canada
Phone: (1) 778 788 41 14
San Francisco
USA
Phone: (1) 415 505 68 28
rodmclean@mac.com
rodmclean.com
Representative:
The Gren Group
thegrengroupinc.com

McVey, Todd
Todd McVey Photography
New York
USA
toddmcveyphotos@gmail.com
toddmcveryphotography.com

Mendes, Marco
> Rodrigues, Márcio

Migs
Michael Lee
Unit 4G Yee Fung Building, 1 Village Road
N/A Hong Kong
China
Phone: (852) 94 49 88 29
migs@migsfoto.com
migsfoto.com
Representative USA:
Glossreps
Holger Kurt Ward
holger@glossreps.com

Miller, Joel Micah
Joel Micah Miller
Photography & Moving Images
Kleine Koenigstraße 1
70178 Stuttgart
Germany
Phone: (49) 711 99 78 19 69
joel-miller.net
studio@joel-miller.net
Representative Germany:
Christa Klubert Photographers
Phone: (49) 211 95 59 64 01
mail@christaklubert.com
christaklubert.com

Molnar, Patrick
443 Lakeshore Dr. NE
30307 Atlanta
USA
Phone: (1) 404 431 83 83
pat@patmolnar.com
patmolnar.com
Representative:
Cynthia Held
cynthiaheld.com

Moodie, Craig
Craig Moodie Photography Pty Ltd
Suite 104, 26-30 Rokeby Street
Collingwood
3066 Melbourne
Australia
Phone: (61) 419 557 443
craig@craigmoodie.com
craigmoodie.com

Morgenstern, Claus
Werftstrasse 15-17
68159 Mannheim
Germany
Phone: (49) 177 347 13 83
info@clausmorgenstern.com
clausmorgenstern.com

Mueller, Adrian
636 Broadway, 8th Floor
10012 New York
USA
Phone: (1) 917 449 24 17
adrian@amueller.com
amueller.com
Representative:
Elizabeth Pojé + Associates
elizabethpoje.com

Mueller, Florian W.
Florian W. Mueller Photography
Otterweg 13
50859 Cologne
Germany
Phone: (49) 175 206 94 71
mail@florianwmueller.com
florianwmueller.com

Muna, RJ
2055 Bryant Street
94110 San Francisco
USA
Phone: (1) 415 285 83 00
studio@rjmuna.com
rjmuna.com
Representative:
Marianne Campbell Associates
mariannecampbell.com

Musilek, Stan
Musilek Inc
1224 Mariposa Street
94107 San Francisco
USA
Phone: (1) 415 621 53 36
57 rue de la Roquette
75011 Paris
France
Phone: (33) 6 30 13 35 04
studio@musilek.com
musilek.com

Müller, Tim
Dorina Lücke
Germany
Phone: (49) 176 22 03 38 18
mail@tim-mueller.com
tim-mueller.com
Representative New York,
Los Angeles, London: cake-factory
Phone: (1) 212 337 36 63
cakefactory.com
Representative Amsterdam,
The Netherlands: Foto Formation
Phone: (31) 20 422 17 08
fotoformation.com

Myers, Tadd
Tadd Myers Photographer
1527 W. State Hwy. 114, ste 500
76051 Grapevine
USA
Phone: (1) 214 752 23 72
hello@taddmyers.com
taddmyers.com

Nagy, Tom
Hofweg 49
22085 Hamburg
Germany
Phone: (49) 40 460 900 93
tn@tomnagy.com
tomnagy.com
Representative New York:
Bernstein & Andriulli
Phone: (1) 212 682 14 90
ba-reps.com
Representative London:
Bernstein & Andriulli
Phone: (44) 207 645 33 39
ba-reps.com
Representative Hamburg:
Marlene Ohlsson
Phone: (49) 40 401 40 50
ohlsson.de

Neibert, Dana
Dana Neibert Photography
826 Orange Ave, #474
92118 Coronado
USA
Phone: (1) 818 558 12 25
info@dananeibert.com
dananeibert.com
Fox Creative
foxcreative.net

Newell, Lennette
Lennette Newell Photography
San Francisco
USA
Phone: (1) 925 930 92 29
mail@lennettenewell.com
lennettenewell.com

Nimmesgern, Stefan
Studio Munich South
Sterzenweg 20
82541 Ammerland
am Starnberger See
Germany
Phone: (49) 171 346 40 65
stefan@nimmesgern.de
nimmesgern.de
Representative:
Silke Lauenstein
Hamburg
Phone: (49) 172 950 26 55

Oldbaby
Gran via 5
28013 Madrid
Spain
Phone: (34) 634 797 888
oldbabyart@gmail.com
oldbaby.cargo.site

Opitz, Bernd
Müggenkampstr. 14A
20257 Hamburg
Germany
Phone: (49) 40 43 19 77 41
mail@berndopitz.com
berndopitz.com
Representative:
Agentur Neubauer
Am Münchfeld 40
80999 München
Germany
Phone: (49) 89 27 29 40 60
info@agenturneubauer.com
agenturneubauer.com

Oppenländer, Peter
Peter Oppenländer Fotodesign
Heinrich-Küderli-Str. 62
71332 Waiblingen
Germany
Phone: (49) 71 51 53 456
oppenlaender@peter-oppenlaender.de
peter-oppenlaender.de

Peachey, Hugh
Blackfactory
Studio 8/ 167 Beavers rd,
Northcote 3070
Melbourne
Australia
Phone: (61) 421 319 291
hugh@hughpeachey.com
hughpeachey.com

Peterson, Bruce
21 Wormwood Street #209
2210 Boston
USA
Phone: (1) 617 292 99 22
bruce@brucepeterson.com
brucepeterson.com

Petrulaitis, Darius
A. Vivulskio st. 27-8
03114 Vilnius
Lithuania
Phone: (370) 699 99 161
darius@petrulaitis.lt
petrulaitis.lt

Pham, Frank
Phamous Photography
Anwar-El-Sadat-Str. 9
70376 Stuttgart
Germany
Phone: (49) 171 48 29 118
frank.pham@hotmail.de
phamousphotography.de

Puente, Jorge
Madrid
Spain
Phone: (34) 616 36 26 15
info@jorgepuente.com
jorgepuente.com

Puschmann, Simon
Roepraredder 34
21031 Hamburg
Germany
Phone: (49) 172 410 65 17
simon@simonpuschmann.com
simonpuschmann.com
Representative UK:
Crxss Agency
John Cross
Phone: (44) 79 70 42 14 35
john@crxss.agency
Representative France:
Bureau de Victor
Carlos Simao
Phone: (33) 1 45 08 84 82
bureaudevictor@wanadoo.fr
Representative USA:
Brite Productions
Matt Nycz
Phone: (1) 212 481 17 20
matt@briteproductions.net
Representative Mexico:
Hero Films
Pablo Herrero
Phone: (52) 55 6725 50 60
pablo@hero-films.com
represented in Germany by myself

Index

Pye, Spid
Spid Pye
57A Cameron Street
Onehunga, Auckland 1061
New Zealand
Phone: (64) 217 24 217
shoot@spid.co.nz
spid.co.nz

Radigonda, Tosca
Austin
USA
Phone: (1) 512 799 79 73
tosca@toscaradigonda.com
toscaradigonda.com

Rave, Manfred
Rave Fotodesign GmbH
Mauritiussteinweg 62
50676 Cologne
Germany
Phone: (49) 221 92 44 20
info@ravefotodesgn.de
ravefotodesgn.de

Reed, Felix
Via del Milliario, 44
40133 Bologna
Italy
Phone: (39) 340 672 61 14
felix@felixreed.com
felixreed.com
Representative Italy:
Sfera Production
Phone: (39) 342 666 52 77
miky@sferaproduction.com

Reimer, Jørgen
Jørgen Reimer AB
Breitenfeltsgatan 8
115 24 Stockholm
Sweden
Phone: (46) 70 77 90 645
jorgen@jorgenreimer.com
jorgenreimer.com

Rice, Sean C.
1536 W 25th St., #129
90732 San Pedro
USA
Phone: (323) 385 19 01
sean.c.rice@gmail.com
seancrice.com
Representative:
Tim Mitchell Artist Representative
tmar-auto.com

Richter, Maren
Maren Richter Photography
Karwinskistraße 52
81247 Munich
Germany
Phone: (49) 170 48 100 99
info@marenrichter.com
marenrichter.com

Robert, Normand
USA
Phone: (1) 514 774 73 10
info@normandrobert.com
normandrobert.com

Robinson, Sam
London & New York
Paper Mill Studios, 9 City Garden Row
London N1 8DW
UK
Phone: (44) 20 7780 7499
23 Meadow Street Studio 4
Brooklyn NY 11206
USA
Phone: (1) 917 675 4993
info@sam-robinson.com
sam-robinson.com
Representative UK:
We Folk
wefolk.com
Representative USA:
Art Department
art-dept.com

Rodrigues, Márcio + Mendes, Marco
Márcio Rodrigues
Lumini Fotografia
Rua Parentins, 321, Santa Lúcia
31160-250 Belo Horizonte
Brazil
Phone: (55) 31 33 37 00 05
lumini@luminifotografia.com.br
luminifotografia.com.br

Rogers, Christy Lee
Nashville, Tennessee
Kailua, Hawaii
USA
christyleerogers@gmail.com
christyleerogers.com

Romer, Stephan
Romer Photography
Platanenstraße 16
40233 Düsseldorf
Germany
Phone: (49) 171 32 57 133
stephan@romerphotography.com
romerphotography.com

Ruíz, Daniel
Representative:
Enrique Gonzales Wilches
DrMarketing
Carrera 15 # 93a-85 Of. 401
110221 Bogotá
Colombia
Phone: (57) 312 376 1996
Juan@drmarketing.com.co
drmarketing.com.co

Salafia, David
USA
Phone: (1) 617 388 12 91
david@davidsalafia.com
davidsalafiaphotography.com

Sappert, Stefan
Vienna
Austria
Phone: (43) 664 51 72 007
studio@stefansappert.com
stefansappert.com
Representative:
Philly Reps
Stacy Swiderski
stacy@phillyreps.com

Sauer, Eberhard
Studio Eberhard Sauer
Rigipsstraße 27
71083 Herrenberg bei Stuttgart
Germany
Phone: (49) 7032 977 00
mail@eberhardsauer.com
eberhardsauer.com

Scharetg, Robb
Scharetg Pictures LLC
6027 Ridge Drive
20816-2645 Bethesda
USA
Phone: (1) 703 209 53 41
robb@scharetgpictures.com
scharetgpictures.com

Schieferecke, Jörg
Representative:
Avenger Photographers
Breisacher Straße 3
81667 Munich
Germany
Phone: (49) 89 614 684 77
sylvia@avenger-photographers.com
avenger-photographers.com

Schinz, Maria
Maria Schinz Imaging
Wittelsbacherstraße 20
80469 München
Germany
Phone: (49) 151 212 68 666
mail@mariaschinz.com
mariaschinz.com

Schlosser, Frederic
Günthersburgallee 47
60316 Frankfurt am Main
Germany
Phone: (49) 176 70 67 42 53
mail@fredericschlosser.de
fredericschlosser.de

Schmidt, Christian
Silberburgstraße 119a
70176 Stuttgart
Germany
Phone: (49) 711 61 511 33
info@christianschmidt.com
christianschmidt.com
Representative Germany:
Claudia Bitzer Fotografenrepräsentanz
cb@claudiabitzer.de
claudiabitzer.de
Representative France:
Wandaprint
hello@wanda.fr
wandaprint.com
Representative USA:
Briteproductions
matt@briteproductions.net
briteproductions.net

Schnabel, Michael
Michael Schnabel Studio
Höhenstrasse 5
73269 Hochdorf
Germany
Phone: (49) 172 73 22 609
mail@michaelschnabel.com
michaelschnabel.com
Representative UK:
Bernstein & Andriulli
London
Phone: (44) 207 645 333 9
Amanda@ba-reps.com
ba-reps.com
Representative USA:
Bernstein & Andriulli
New York
Phone: (1) 212 220 91 69
Phone: (1) 917 975 743 9
kat@ba-reps.com
ba-reps.com
Representative China:
Bernstein & Andriulli
Phone: (86) 138 186 727 35
edie.zhang@amanacliq.com
ba-reps.com

Scharetg, Robb

Representative Australia:
Suits & Sneakers
Phone: (61) 1 300 804 372
Phone: (61) 4 11 10 24 01
anne@suitsandsneakers.global
suitsandsneakers.global

Schultz, Richard
Richard Schultz Productions LLC
5 Stone Tower Lane
02806 Barrington
USA
Phone: (1) 401 289 22 29
richard@rschultz.com
Representative:
BCM
beyondcreativemgmt.com

Schwabe, Kai
Germany
Phone: (49) 151 23 00 19 49
info@kaischwabe.de
kaischwabe.com

Schwalfenberg, Joerg
Joerg Schwalfenberg Photography
Alsterdorfer Strasse 268
22297 Hamburg
Germany
Phone: (49) 40 27 87 80 84
mail@schwalfenberg.eu
corporate-photo.com

Seckler, Zack
New York
USA
zs@zackseckler.com
zackseckler.com
Representative:
Brite Productions

Seguin, Jean-François
Jean-François Seguin Photography
24 Ward street
M6H 4A6 Toronto, Ontario
Canada
Phone: (1) 514 654 92 72
info@jeanfrancoisseguin.com
jeanfrancoisseguin.com

Shank, Niv
8 Strasseman street
10249 Berlin
Germany
Phone: (1) 646 479 87 01
heynivshank@gmail.com
nivshank.com
Representative Italy & China:
1806 agency
info@1806.agency
1806.it
Representative France:
C'est la vie agency
info@cest-lavie.fr
cest-lavie.fr
Representative Spain:
Bamboo
info@bamboobcn.com
bamboobcn.com
Representative Germany:
Kai Tietz
info@kaitietz.de
kaitietz.de

Short, David
UK
Phone: (44) 7973 24 94 54
davidshort-photography.co.uk
Agent gillturner.com

472

Shroff, Madhur
3rd Floor, Alvares House
188, Veer Savarkar Marg
Mumbai
India
Phone: (91) 22 24 44 0427
madhurshroff@yahoo.com
madhurshroff.com

Siegert, Christoph
Photography & Film
Lagerstraße 11, Halle H, 1. OG
20357 Hamburg
Germany
Phone: (49) 40 43 25 20 90
studio@christoph-siegert.com
christoph-siegert.com

Sigal, Martin
Catamarca 2165 Martinez
1640 Buenos Aires
Argentina
martin@martinsigal.com
martinsigal.com
Representative USA:
michelle@foureleven.agency
foureleven.agency
@foureleven_agency
Representative Mexico:
info@ntproducciones.com
kristian@ntproducciones.com
ntproducciones.com
Representative Colombia-Panama:
claudiaguerra@ochurus.com
ochurus.com

simon+kim
Kim Sokola, Simon Bolzern
simon+kim werbefotografie.ch
Kreuzstrassse 34
6010 Kriens
Switzerland
Phone: (41) 41 340 82 70
kim@werbefotografie.ch
simonandkim.work

Siu, Lindsay
Lindsay Siu Photographer
220 Victoria Drive, Unit 180
V5L 0C7 Vancouver
Canada
Phone: (1) 604 780 47 55
info@lindsaysiu.com
lindsaysiu.com
Representative:
Dictionary Films
dictionaryfilms.com

Smith, Chris Frazer
London
UK
Phone: (44) 07 831 37 66 87
chris@chrisfrazersmith.com
chrisfrazersmith.com

Sokolovski, Dejan
Dejan Sokolovski Photography AB
Ekängsgatan 49
506 48 Borås
Sweden
Phone: (46) 76 221 30 76
me@dejansokolovski.com
dejansokolovski.com
photoagency.se
Represantive USA:
Holger Kurt Ward, Gloss Reps
glossreps.com

Stableford, Tyler
Tyler Stableford Productions
46 Weant Blvd
Carbondale
USA
Phone: (1) 970 319 90 09
tyler@tylerstableford.com
tylerstableford.com

Stamenis, Nikiforos
Souidias 103
28100, Argostoli, Kefalonia
Greece
Phone: (30) 69 42 01 58 60
info@stamenisnikiforos.gr
stamenisnikiforos.gr

Steinheisser, Wolf-Peter
wpsteinheisser photography
Kurfürstenstraße 22
71636 Ludwigsburg
Germany
Phone: (49) 172 63 51 041
wp@wpsteinheisser.com
wpsteinheisser.com

Stinson, David
David Stinson Photography
Atlanta
USA
david@davidstinson.com
davidstinsonphoto.com

Stock, Simon
London
UK
Phone: (44) 78 50 70 74 75
simonstock.com
Representatives UK:
Jamie Stephens Represents
jsragency.com
Representatives USA:
Greenhouse Reps
greenhousereps.com

Straley, Chris
Chris Straley Photographs
1722 South Coast Highway Suite 1
Oceanside, CA 92054
USA
Phone: (1) 760 390 39 04
chris@chrisstraley.com
chrisstraley.com
Representative:
Fox Creative
foxcreative.net

Streiber, Art
Art Streiber Photography
2239 Camden Avenue
90064 Los Angeles
USA
Phone: (1) 310 473 41 08
studio@artstreiber.com
Representative:
Giant Artists
giantartists.com

Summers, Braden
Braden Summers Photography
Los Angeles
USA
Phone: (1) 860 490 14 67
braden@bradensummers.com
bradensummers.com
Representative:
Tidepool Reps
tidepoolreps.com

Sutton, Tim
TMS Productions
90813 Long Beach
USA
Phone: (1) 310 908 2989
tim@timsuttonphoto.com
timsuttonphoto.com

Tacevski, Goran
Glad s.r.o. , Tacevski s.r.o.
Butovicka 10
15000 Prague
Czech Republic
Phone: (420) 602 282 557
goran@glad.studio
goran@tacevski.com
glad.studio
tacevski.com

Tadder, Tim
Tim Tadder Photography
1393 Caudor St.
92024 Encinitas, CA
USA
Phone: (1) 760 632 66 39
mail@timtadder.com
timtadder.com
Representative:
Heather Elder Represents
heatherelder.com

Tamboly, Armand
Tamboly Photodesign
Berlin / Gothenburg
Germany / Sweden
Phone: (49) 15 22 93 44 899
info@tambolydesign.com
tambolydesign.com

Telfer, Alex
Alex Telfer Photography
Kingsland Church Studios,
NE62DW Newcastle Upon Tyne
UK
Phone: (44) 191 265 73 84
alex@alextelfer.com, alextelfer.com
Representative UK:
Peter Bailey Company
Phone: (44) 207 935 26 26
peter@peterbailey.co.uk
peterbailey.co.uk
Representative USA:
i2i photography
Phone: (1) 212 925 54 10
frank@i2iphoto.com
i2iphoto.com
Representative France:
Ask Our Agents
Phone: (33) 142 74 42 75
florence@askouragents.fr
askouragents.fr
Representative Germany:
Severin Wendeler
Phone: (49) 40 800 80 99 99
office@severinwendeler.com
severinwendeler.de
Representative Italy:
Mandala Creative Productions
Phone: (39) 02 366 35 750
info@mandalacp.it
mandalacp.it

Terada, Tomoya
3S
301 saito building
Kyomachibori 2-2-3 Nishi-Ku
550-0003 Osaka
Japan
Phone: (81) 6 61 36 70 82
info@3s-photo.com
3s-photo.com

The Voorhes
4312 Gillis
78745 Austin, Texas
USA
Phone: (1) 512 386 74 17
adam@voorhes.com
voorhes.com
Representative:
Candace Gelman & Associates
candacegelman.com

Thompson III, Richard
Los Angeles
USA
rvt3.net
Representative:
Brite Productions
Phone: (1) 212 481 17 20
briteproductions.net

Thorp, Graham
London
UK
Phone: (44) 77 78 26 52 05
graham@grahamthorp.com
Representative:
Create Agency
arnold@create.agency
Phone: (31) 40 78 77 126
Mobile: (31) 6 22 79 89 33

Todon, Dave
Instil Image Co.
Toronto
Canada
Phone: (1) 416 596 65 87
pamela@instilimageco.com
instilimageco.com
Representative:
M Represents
mrepresents.com

Tot, Klaudia
Klaudia Tot Photography
Libanonstraße 66
70184 Stuttgart
Germany
Phone: (49) 151 124 01 005
mail@klaudiatot.com
klaudiatot.com

Tracy + David
Tracy + David Stills and Motion
Los Angeles
USA
Phone: (1) 949 525 797
hello@tracydavid.com
tracydavid.com

Trautmann, Marc
Lindleystraße 4
60314 Frankfurt am Main
Germany
Phone: (49) 171 342 89 41
info@marctrautmann.com
marctrautmann.com
Representative:
Schierke Artists
schierke.com
Baader Straße 15
80469 München
Representative USA:
We are Casey
CASEY Creative Group LTD.
Phone: (1) 212 858 37 57
info@wearecasey.com

Traylor, Bryan
Locker14 Films & Photography
PO BOX 32022, Camps Bay
RSA 8040, Cape Town
South Africa
Phone: (27) 82 222 56 23
bryan@locker14.com
locker14.com

Index